FRANKENSTEIN DIARIES
The Romantics

The Secret Memoirs of Mary Shelley

By Mary Wollstonecraft Shelley
and Michael January

Frankenstein Diaries: The Romantics
The Secret Memoirs of Mary Shelley

Winged Lion Publications

Library of Congress Cataloging on Request
ISBN-13: 978-0692429716

"I saw a pale student of unhallowed arts kneeling beside the thing he had created. The hideous phantasm of a man stretched out, and then, on the working of some powerful engine, show signs of life and stir."

"Frightful must it be—of any human endeavor to mock the stupendous mechanism of the Creator of the world."

Frankenstein: or, The New Prometheus
Mary Wollstonecraft Shelley

Preface

It is now nearly thirty years since these events took place. I endeavored to see the small journal I had kept to be published, encouraged by my husband to offer some notation of our time. The journal was not very copious, due in some matter to my own self-reticence. Now, with a change in circumstance since the long ago passing of my dear friend, I can come to admit that I also was judicious in its editing; I confess to leaving out some portions which I believed at the time to be importune to expose to public scrutiny. In my original text I attempted to describe only the scenery through which we passed, and a few of the individuals in whom we had commerce, but I feel now compelled to expose a few more intimate details and occurrences of interest which I hitherto omitted.

I began what has come to be entitled *History Of A Six Weeks Tour* with the passage, "*We left London July 28th, 1814, on a hotter day than has been known in this climate for many years. I am not a good traveller, and this heat agreed very ill with me, till, on arriving at Dover, I was refreshed by a sea-bath. As we very much wished to cross the channel with all possible speed, we would not wait for the packet of the following day (it being then about four in the afternoon) but hiring a small boat, resolved to make the passage the same evening, the seamen promising us a voyage of two hours."*

With the fullness of time, and the notoriety of my now most popular work in its advanced printing with an added introduction regarding a waking revelation in that summer on Lake Geneva, which I now freely and for the first time admit I deliberately structured to avoid the revelation of some facts I had promised to keep private, I wish to here amend my diary in a more complete form. I will add to the details of that journey some relevant explanation of its cause and of inspirations of my now honored horrific tale of a student of science and his creation, and the origin of that name and title which has until now been only the subject of speculation and mystery. What follows is impossible to document in its entirety, much of it only now reconstituted from my memory, but here in these pages you will discover the truth of the origins, for there are many, of *Frankenstein.*

Mary Wollstonecraft Shelley
Chester Square, London — November, 1848

CHAPTER ONE

Skinner Street

As everything must have a beginning, I had begun my journal in the bowels of that small sailing craft we had engaged at the harbour of Dover to make our passage to France. I had brought some writing paper with the thought to record some details of what I viewed at the age of sixteen to be an adventure, with a desire to experience some remembrance of one I had loved since my first awareness of life, but had never known in flesh. It was undoubtedly a pure imprudence of youth, our escape. Yet, I have never since regretted it on the shape of our lives together, though of its consequence upon others of our sphere, I have.

We had come to the white chalk shore of Dover at great haste with the urging of the four-horse coach from Dartford only a few hours distance ahead of our pursuers, as our intent had been discovered by my enemy within moments of the rising of the sun and the discovery of our absence from our beds. I know in full realization now that it was not for me the expectation of ruin was feared, but for her whom I had convinced to accompany us. Yet, before I begin the events of our journey, let me step back to an earlier day to illustrate how we had come to this fearful, and yet wonderful, irreversible moment in the progress of our lives.

It was my first glimpse of Shelley since my return from Scotland, presented though a cloud of acrid smoke in the parlour of my father's book shop, wherein this story has its true beginning. He was enthralled in a deep discussion of immortality with Mr. Coleridge and Mr. Lamb, two of my father's, Mr. Godwin's, circle of distinguished literary acolytes. It was a clear evening in May of 1814 when I had just returned from a brief, but sadly instructive attendance to a service at the old church in St Pancras with my step-sister Claire. I shall call her Claire throughout this narrative for clarity's sake, though at this point in her life she was known by her true given name of Jane, a subject of some confusion and comity which will soon become of importance.

My father was well known to be no friend to the church in any of its forms, but my recent time in Scotland, among dear companions, had reintroduced me to the practice of kneeling before an image of that force which inhabits the mind of man in dark moments of loss or emptiness. My sister had suggested the experiment, though chiefly, I believe, because she had taken notice of a handsome young vicar there employed, as seemed to be the chief occupation of her mind at fifteen years and a few months of earthly existence. I acquiesced in the adventure for another pleasant look at the sylvan neighborhood I had loved in younger days. It had been at the urging and arrangement of *her* (to whom I refer as little as possible in public breath), we had left Somers Town in Camden, to take up residence in the dirty commercial quarter of Holborn, in the north of London, within a distance walk from the former district, but far removed in character.

The sign above the book shop and publishing concern presented *her* name, and only tangentially by inference my father, reading *M. J. Godwin & Co. Juvenile Library*. The public portion of the concern took up the lower two rooms of connected row houses with a large latticed window facing the narrow confines of Skinner Street at No. 41. The back lower rooms housed book binding equipment and packing tables, while the upstairs warren of joined rooms provided our living quarters. She had persuaded my father that children's books were of more an economic value than the deeper works of his own vision, with the argument that there will always be a new batch of children born to the middle classes to read, while the education needed to understand the broad philosophical concepts of his interests were only available to the class of society less likely to pass by a window display. Though, it was my opinion that it was not commerce, but her own limited viewpoint that informed her business philosophy. Illustrated children's stories filled the soot-lined frames of the bay window on shelves now barely visible in the dark shadows of gathering gloom.

As Claire and I stood outside the door of Skinner Street, we could see the luminescence of a lamp burning in the window of the parlour above, and could hear a collection of male voices echoing in the street now settled into evening silence. This was not unfamiliar to us, as Mr. Godwin on many occasions had visitors to occupy his energy, some of wide fame who would come to give him their obeisance and respect. Many of his circle he would encounter at the publishing house of Mr. John Murray in Marylebone, at that respected gentleman's "afternoon teas", and would come to Skinner Street to carry into an evening in philosophical discussion, with a more full bodied beverage. I recognized the staccato voice, a stutter tinged with a mirthful crackle, of Mr. Charles Lamb, whom I enjoyed with the fondness of an uncle and the sonorous growl of the sad and compact, Mr. Taylor Coleridge. Yet, the third voice I did not recognize. It was certainly not Mr. Wordsworth, of which I was glad, as he always seemed rather colic and stern to me, and never much interested in seeing children in his presence. It was of a high pitch, youthful in tone, and though not exactly warm by any means, somehow compelling in urgent enthusiasm.

Claire and I crept quietly up the dark stairs to the parlour, removing our coats and untying our bonnets, as such was the fashion we had adopted. We stood at the top of the stair steps without announcing our presence and unseen by the four men in the room. They were situated as usual in chairs gathered in a circular arrangement. Brandies in snifters for each were on a small table, with one oil lamp burning for light, which cast huge ghostly shadows on the bookshelves of haphazardly arranged volumes about the octagonal cornered walls of the room. A red coal and peat fire glowed in the iron grate of the hearth, with an occasional crackle of the moss which provided a grey pallor to the room.

A thread-worn oriental carpet only covered the center of the room, mostly under father's feet as he leaned back in his centrally placed stuffed chair of unintentionally comic side wings. The whale oil lamp shone with a gleam on the round space of father's forehead where hair had once inhabited, it being unfortunate for him that wigs had fallen from favor, except for the footmen and servants of great manors, and a few aging stalwarts one might see passing on an avenue. The two gentlemen of middle-age I knew well, but the young man who rested uneasily on the chair opposite to me, was for a moment unfamiliar; but yet, not so. I had seen him once before, when he had come to dinner with his pretty wife. I then instantly knew who he was from the descriptions in my elder sister, Fanny's, effusive letters. It must be indeed Mr. Percy Shelley. Why had I not recognized him? Had he changed so much? Or had I? I suppose that now, after nearly two years away, between the ages of fourteen and sixteen, my perception of many things may have changed.

He was handsome, though thin and tall, with a tousled reddish-blond cluft of curled hair slightly off-balance on his head with an unruly length. His arms at the bony wrists seemed to have a naturally wan and freckled complexion, but his face was darkened by sunlight, with eyes of blue which pierced the smoke haze. He leaned a bit forward in his chair as if he might leap off it at the drop of a pin, yet, remained in absolute stillness as he focused on the conversation about him, seeming to hold his own comment in secret to himself, until it might be revealed. Curiously, he did not acknowledge or register the slightest indication of seeing me, though his view of the room was directly opposite the stair where Claire and I could not have been invisible in our afternoon dresses of cheerful color, even in the faint gloom of the oil lamp.

"Murray has asked me to perform a translation of Johann Goethe's Dr. Faustus." It was Coleridge who spoke. He had known father for some years now, and always looked to me in perpetual pain. His habituation to laudanum was obvious to anyone who knew him, and it had served to cause him near constant discomfort in his bowels at this stage in his life, the age of forty-two, unable to remain in any one position for more than a few minutes at a time.

"Is your German that g-good?" wondered Lamb, with a wink to Godwin, "the language of cat-monkeys to my ears. All consonants and no vowels, with the end of the sentence at the beginning and no idea what anyone is saying until they've stopped inexplicably."

Charles Lamb was only a few years junior to Coleridge, a great poet in his own right, but now most known for the children's version of Shakespeare he had published though my father's and step-mother's imprimatur, written with his sister, Mary.

Dear Mr. Lamb, for that he was to me, had written his early poems while confined in a madhouse, and his sister had also been resident in the same after having killed their mother with a kitchen paring knife while peeling some carrots for supper and engaging in an argument over the contents of a soup.

His stutter prevented him from the stage reading performances which had brought Coleridge to public notoriety for his lectures on the bard of Stratford-Upon-Avon, leaving Lamb to insist the plays were better to be read than performed.

"It's not my German, but my English which I fear may fail me," Coleridge grumbled. "How do you translate a vocabulary of five thousand words? Shakespeare only had three-thousand to write the entire cannon of common English." He shifted his seat again to face my father.

"Byron apparently puts his faith in Murray and receives his payment. What do you think, Godwin? Of Murray, as a publisher?"

"I am glad you're not asking my opinion of Lord Gordon Byron." My dear father's face screwed itself into a sour knot. He had no patience with the now infamous antics of the most notorious romantic figure of our time, *mad, bad, and dangerous to know*, especially after the revelations of his affair with Lady Caroline Lamb, fortunately of no relation to Charles and Mary.

The others laughed, and I noticed that Claire, who had been entirely disinterested in the discussion, had perked up at the mention of the lord poet. She fiddled for no reason whatsoever with a stray thread on her dress and gazed across the room at Shelley. She had written to me of his visits to Skinner Street in my absence with some effusion, and had referenced at length my elder sister's enthusiastic response to his attentions, but since Lord Byron's thrust into notoriety, her interest had shifted. Afterward, it was only excerpts from society news of Mr. Byron's reported habits which seemed to fill her letters. Claire had been born Jane, but like her mother, seemed to have no loyalty to supported fact. She had decided she wanted to be called Claire after beginning her studies in French, yet on occasion, wished to be addressed as Clara, when she felt like admitting to English heritage.

"He's beautiful, isn't he?" She whispered to me, covering her lips with her fingers. "It's no wonder Fanny can't stop herself. But I've lost interest." My step-sister's manner could be infectious at times, but her feigned aloofness in her attention to the young man across the room was unconvincing. Her gaze was as unrestrained as I later suspected was mine.

Percy Bysshe Shelley was twenty-one years of age when we met on this occasion. He was the eldest son of a baronet from West Sussex. His grandfather, Sir Bysshe Shelley, had been born in colonial New Jersey in the Americas and had purchased his Baronetcy, established through blood connection by marriage to a descendant to Henry VII, and had built himself an estate in Sussex on the sea coast. Shelley's grandfather was still alive and his title had yet to pass to his father, so that Percy was twice removed from a lordship he would never receive.

"Murray has a solid reputation," Godwin offered, "but for German, you may speak to my wife, as she has managed with it. In fact, we are in correspondence regarding a translation of the Grimm stories."

Lamb was incredulous, "As a children's b-book?! Shoving mothers into ovens?! Wolves eating children? Imagine the nightmares!"

"I'm looking forward to them," I heard my own voice, though I had to that point no intention of joining the conversation. "I've only heard details of some of the stories— And I have to say, I relish a good nightmare, as long as I awake."

"Mary—" Godwin now saw us behind him. Lamb and Coleridge arose from their chairs, setting aside their brandies. Lamb stepped over to me to give me a familiar embrace. He looked at our clothes, distilling at once from where we had come.

"You've been to church!' he said with a hint of bemusement. "Don't worry, I won't say anything in a room of the resolutely Godless."

"Mr. Lamb." I smiled at him, as I could not help it.

My father gestured with a circular wave, by way of introduction. "Coleridge, Mr. Percy Shelley, my middle daughter, Mary, you may have met, and my youngest by Mrs. Clairmont, Jane."

Claire curtsied, with a bit of a coquettish grin while correcting him, "Claire. Gentlemen." Her insistence on a name of her own fantasy caused my father to wince at the imprudence of having fathered daughters.

"Mary's just returned from Scotland," he explained for those unaware of my travels, "in the care of Mr. Baxter, whom I asked she be brought up like a philosopher—or rather a cynic."

"A Calvinist cynic?!" barked Coleridge. "She doesn't get enough anarchy at home?" He was only half-joking at what he knew of the preferred temper of the Scottish Presbyterian rite. The others laughed, but he looked suddenly ill, touching his forehead, "I must sit."

As he sat down again in a new position, I caught Shelley now looking at me steadfastly, as an owl might study a dove. I was myself unable to look away, until Claire tugged at my sleeve and I could see my father noticing us.

"They'll go on all night," Claire whispered.

"We're disturbing your conversation," I said politely, preparing to leave, though I ached to stay.

Claire curtsied and turned to the hallway which led to the rest of the house and our bedroom. I started to follow a step behind, but I heard the scrape of a chair behind me and Shelley's voice.

"Perhaps—Miss Godwin might be allowed to linger? If she has no fear of night terrors?"

I turned to see him, standing at his chair, with a slight tilt, as if the room might be the deck of a ship run-aground.

"May I stay?" I asked of father.

Mr. Lamb offered me his chair, but I noticed a stool in the corner, taking it instead.

Claire paused in the hallway, fixing me with a sharp approbation, then turned and vanished into the black maw of the hallway.

"I only wish to be a fly on the wall," I demurred as I perched on it, but indeed I wished for so much more. I had discovered the richness of books and was curious of the mysteries of the world, and here within these walls, barely an arm's length distance, were some of my country's brightest of minds, in what was to them but casual conversation, but to me, a window.

"Well, it's not Goethe's language I take issue with in any case. I'm just not sure I can live with flying devils on rum pots for five months. Alchemy. Immortality. Selling your soul." He seemed genuinely at a loss to embrace the subject of Goethe's play about a doctor selling his soul for knowledge, with witches and poisonous love potions.

"More your themes than mine, Shelley," he addressed the younger man, so far silent. "I thought your St. Irvyne was marvelous stuff. The Rosy Cross and secret societies—"

"Perhaps we could republish your Rosicrucian story, Shelley," offered Godwin. "Under your own name this round, rather than 'a Gentleman from Oxford'. If you might advance printing costs—"

The subject of money was bound to occur, as was the recurrent nature of my father's relationship to Shelley. Shelley's work, *St Irvyne, or The Rosicrucian*, a story of a wandering outcast who encounters an alchemist seeking the secret of immortality to revive a love he had lost to death, published with what he assumed would be anonymity while still at college in Oxford, had been inspired by a thematic reverie of my father's, but distinguished by his own view and knowledge of far off places my father had never encountered. Coleridge and Lamb looked discomfited.

Coleridge kindly changed the subject. "I've noticed a fair share of Godwin's cant in your public positions, Shelley. Your letter to Lord Ellenborough pleading for Eaton's trial for atheism—" He made a silent cough, more a spasm, seeming in pain. "Excuse me," he pleaded, reaching into his breast coat pocket to retrieve a small dark bottle. It held a glass dropper tube with a stopper. He removed the tube, drawing some of the dark reddish brown liquid from the bottle with his blackened fingertip over the tube end and dropped the liquid onto his blackened tongue, I imagined not unlike a victim of the medieval plague. His nearly hourly dose of laudanum, which a physician had convinced him to take in small increments rather than single doses, was a constant and familiar ritual to his friends.

Lamb continued for him, being of a common mind and curiosity, "Yes, you argued, so eloquently, for the right of freedom of Mr. Eaton to express his opinion in the press that he was not denying the existence of God, but that Scripture should be open to reason."

"It still did not save his conviction for 'blasphemous libel'", answered Shelley, with a flick of wry bemusement. Shelley's letter to a justice in support of Lord Eaton, had declared his own views of the question of the existence of God, fully in public view, for which he would pay many penalties.

"How can you libel an ephemeral being who only exists in a book?" Shelley reasoned. "Despite my entreaty, Mr. Eaton still rots in confinement, convicted of libel—against God. These are the same views, I am afraid, that have put me so distant from my father. Little good my letter did."

Coleridge drifted a bit as the laudanum took its effect. "Immortality," he mused. "Life beyond the living of it. Do you know that in Newgate Prison, even as we sit here, they are experimenting with bringing the dead back to life?"

"Propaganda!" Lamb injected, not believing it

"No. I have seen it. A medical friend is involved." Coleridge leaned forward, as if to make a full confession. "They have taken to heart the theories of the Italian, Galvani, who reanimated tissue by passing an electrical charge through a muscle of the groin."

Lamb nodded. "Yes. On f-frogs. I've read it."

"We pretend to play God—" Coleridge roared suddenly as if to a room of breadth and depth. "These madmen, who think themselves guardians of health are applying electricity to the bodies of hanged prisoners, in efforts to spark them back to life! Diabolical!"

I had never heard such a discussion, but the ideas and arguments flashed in my brain like charges of animating energy.

"Criminals who never die?" Shelley caught my distracted gaze with a smirk at his joke, and fixed on me with an intense interest I could not avoid.

Coleridge continued, regaining his somber opiate mood. "Absolutely ghoulish. The next thing you know, they'll be digging up dead bodies from graves for their medical fancies, to assemble into Herculean protomen!"

Shelley suddenly leaped to his feet, as if an electrical charge had jolted him. He circled the room behind the chairs, stalking about like an uncontainable dynamo. He whirled his hand like winding a crank.

"Electricity! In batteries!" He said it as if it was a revelation, continuing his circle about the room. I could not help but watch him with a transfixed fascination, this energy bound into one human being.

"At school, I used a friction electrical charge attached to my door handle, a small revenge against the bullies who tormented me. Mad Shelley! They called me. Mad Shelley!" he exclaimed with a certain pride. "One day, electricity, from great farms of batteries, will free mankind from toil. It will power our cities. It will operate machines which now must be driven by coal fires and steam. It will wash the dirt from our window sills and streets and clear our acrid urban air. Then, once free from labour, we can while our time in study of nature and the human soul!"

Still miming his electrical crank, he ended abruptly in front of me. I looked up into his face at its marked enthusiasm and his amazing vision. I laughed, but softly, for my mirth was not at him, but still caused by him. He smiled, a small return, allowing the imaginary crank to fall from his hand.

"Mad Shelley still," Lamb mused in remembrance of his own youth, looking at us.

The mood stopped as a heavy spirit entered the room; a dark shape was in partial shadow at the edge of the lamp's glow.

"This is unacceptable." Mary Jane Godwin glared disapprovingly at me in the midst of the company. She stepped further into the light, a stolid and wide package of a woman in dreary black, with a pale complexion, except for a perpetual rouge about the cheeks under a brown mob of hair, tortured into a bun. Mrs. Clairmont, as I preferred to call her, my father's second wife after the death of my own mother, had played upon his grief and induced him into matrimony, I am convinced, by her desire for the value of his reputation and played upon his grief.

Lamb turned to the shadow in the doorway with a courteous formal demure, for he, too, did not like her. "Mrs. Godwin, please, the fault is ours. We are dissolute old masters needing the attention of a vibrant generation for an audience."

I avoided looking at my step-mother in the least and directly addressed Mr. Lamb. "It is Mrs. Clairmont who decides who receives attention, and who does not, in this house." I curtsied to signal a polite, but I admit, abrupt intended departure. "Thank you, Mr. Lamb, for the defense. Father. Mr. Shelley—"

"*Sweet slumber, steal o'er sensation and give that faithful bosom joy, to catch light, life and rapture from her smile*—", he said in a soft voice.

I recognized the passage, and I'm afraid it must have caused a slight warming of my cheeks.

"Ianthe," I acknowledged with a smile, for it was a passage from his well-received and most marvelous *Queen Mab* and Ianthe, the sweet object of its idyllic fairy world reft by the jealousy of the aging Mab.

"Off, now," said Mab (for *she* was that nemesis in my regard) thus ordered from the intellectual light of that room. I fixed her with an intense gaze of my antipathy, for it was my custom at that age, unable to express my true feelings toward her. I left my friends to reenter the darkness of the hallway and to bed. As I went, I could hear her behind, offering some smoked sturgeon as hostess.

"Going," said Coleridge, rising from his chair with discomfort, at the furniture and the company.

"It's late." Lamb agreed, downing the last of his brandy glass, while they quickly collected their coats.

"Percy, might you stay a moment?" Godwin asked in a tone of forced casualness.

Coleridge and Lamb exchanged glances, knowing what discussion was on tap. They nodded goodnight and headed down the stairs. Godwin waited until they were gone and his wife faded again into the darkness for some feigned chore.

Shelley braced himself for what he knew was coming. I heard this from him at some later time, for he was always forthright with me in matters of my family.

"I know I have prevailed upon you in the past," said Godwin, "yet, I may ask again for a loan. Business—"

Shelley was hesitant to be brusque, as it was he who had opened this door.

"Please, Godwin, these are not loans. I'm no banker. I write—yet I have no craving to pen writs for debtors' prison. Even if that is to be my fate—"

He glanced down the darkened hallway, drawn by a desire to visit again. "Truly, I owe you much favor. For you have shaped my thoughts, and I owe you for the light of justice your work has brought on this world."

It was Shelley who had originally written to my father, a stranger to him, known only by his philosophical and radical ideas which Shelley wished to understand and develop with his own thoughts. He had offered to assist Godwin in matters of expense as he felt was the duty of the well-situated to advance the artist, but father's need grew to dependence, just as Coleridge's regular draught of narcotic had imprisoned him. Shelley, while still desirous of holding to his professed creed and his discovered personal interest in Godwin's familial household, had found himself in a complicated maze of his own finances. Denied his allowance by his father, who objected to that very philosophy which would support Godwin, and his full inheritance yet to come to him while his grandfather was still in life spirit, and supporting a wife and child, Shelley had been forced to borrow his own living from kind friends of fortune, with the expectation they would be made whole again once his full estate was gained.

"I will scrape my accounts and carry you a bit further, Godwin," he offered. "But I may need to bring it in small increments."

Father shook his hand heartily, grateful for the relief of doubt. Though, his gratefulness would soon be challenged by the events to follow which would affect all our lives for eternity.

"That's all I can ask," he said.

~~~

CHAPTER TWO

Fanny

It was nearly the last time I would see my dear sister, Fanny. For it was she, I believe, who was the most innocent in all the events which tumbled like a hillside of loose slipping shale in our tragic story. I hesitate to think of it as a tragedy, for it was full of so much beauty and joy, yet the twists of a tragic fate did intrude upon it, and Fanny was one of its recipients.

It was Fanny as well from whom my animosity toward my enemy also felt its sharpest jolt. Her full name, as it is a feature of our story that we are defined both in familial identity and in complexity of feeling by our names, was Francis Imlay Godwin. At twenty, she was four years beyond me and the only child who had known my mother. She was in truth only my half-sister, as we are all only of partial connection to one another, but I could not feel a closer kinship than if we were one. She was the child of my mother and an American named Imlay, whom my mother had known and loved while in France. It was during the revolution in bloody turmoil they had romanced, and sweet Fanny was the result. They had attempted to marry while in that country by registration with the American consulate, but that marriage was not recognized by British standard, so that Fanny was, at best, unofficial in the eyes of a society based on lines of parentage.

Fanny was not pretty, but I would offer her as winsome, as I believe her soul held a beauty that shone through the scars of her childhood illness. Small-pox, if survived, always marked its host with a badge of that momentous battle and Fanny's was by fortune only present from her throat to the lower part of her cheek. But it could not be avoided in a mirror.

She was rearranging a stack of books in the shop as I watched her efficiency. Father and Mrs. Clairmont had come to rely on her industry to manage their business affairs, father being too crowded by his intellectual reveries to be so practical in accounting, and the she-devil, too absorbed by the care of her own children to be loving.

"Mrs. Godwin is intent on sending me to Ireland for the summer. She says it's for my health, but I think she's afraid I am too keen on Mr. Shelley's attentions," Fanny said as she straightened a volume of cross-hatch word puzzles. "He has been coming around more so, since you've come home."

I could not answer her directly. I knew well her feeling for him, as he had indeed paid her much court while I was away, mostly unknown to him in my youth. But since our meeting in that smoky parlour, not scarce a month gone by now, Shelley had become a regular attendant at Skinner Street, but not to dote on Fanny, as had been his habit before. He was fond of her, I truly believe, but it was me upon whom his attention was now fixed.

I focused on browsing through titles of the shop to see what new had been added. Our conversation was reserved as there were customers, in the shape of a mother with two of her children, also browsing the offerings. The children seemed to delight in some drawings of elfish creatures in a fantasy taken from Mr. Spenser's *The Faerie Queen*.

"She means for me to depart when she has finished her translation of the Swiss Family Robinson," Fanny said with an earnest acceptance, while reserving some hidden emotion.

Mrs. Clairmont (I call her still, as *Mrs. Godwin* for me shall always remain another) had found some success in juvenile literature by advertising in foreign publishing journals for works in other languages, French and German, both with which she was familiar. She had also prevailed through contacts of my father among authors with a reputation which stood chiefly on the success of the Lambs' juvenile *Shakespeare*, which had brought the Elizabethan dramatist some return to favor and rediscovery, after having been relegated as old fashioned and obsolete by in the enlightened age. The *Swiss Family Robinson* would become one of her most widely known acquisitions as a publisher and she was endeavoring at the time to persuade the Brothers Grimm to allow her to translate their works. This effort would involve repeated correspondence, principally with one of the brothers, I do not recall which one however, but would be unsuccessful in the acquisition.

"Where are mother's *Original Stories*?!" I asked with some intensity, as I was shocked not to find them anywhere in sight. Fanny was silent, as she was more accustomed to diplomacy than I. Of my mother's works of substantial thought and philosophical judgment, her *Original Stories from Real Life* was written for the enlightenment of children and enchantingly illustrated by her friend, Mr. William Blake, and written for Fanny expressly when she was the child mother knew.

"But it is a children's book! She can't expect children to be tainted by it!" I cried out in some heat, as I felt it was a betrayal. "I see father's histories. Rome. England. Greece. His bible stories—" The display was peppered with my father's lengthy detailed historical treatises, published by Mr. Hookham, for which bed time reading was far from the intent, and his books for children, not written under his own name, but as Baldwin.

"But it is a children's book! She can't expect children to be tainted by it!" I cried out in some heat, as I felt it was a betrayal. "I see father's histories. Rome. England. Greece. His bible stories—" The display was peppered with my father's lengthy detailed historical treatises, published by Mr. Hookham, for which bed time reading was far from the intent, and his books for children, not written under his own name, but as Baldwin. I even found among the stacks my father's most provocative work.

"Here is his *Political Justice*! But nothing of my mother's? Has she vanished from the face of the earth? From memory?

"She means for me to depart when she has finished her translation of the Swiss Family Robinson," Fanny said with an earnest acceptance, while reserving some hidden emotion.

The mother with her young children looked over to the ranting young woman among the paper and ink. I tried to regain my dignity, but it was stinging to the core that Mrs. Clairmont would revel in my father's oeuvre, yet of my mother, there was not an inkling.

Fanny looked upon me in uncomfortable sympathy, "She feels father's biography has made her too scandalous a figure."

"She just fears she can't compete, with her translations—for father's affections—"

"Be fair, Mary. Be kind."

I went to my sister to embrace her, for I knew it was she who was more victim than I. Yet, she bore it with far more grace that I could ever imagine of myself. And though I blamed my step-mother for her ill treatment of a dear memory, when she could have nurtured it while still having care of her own, for the capacity to love is not divided by payments of it, it was my father who had been at unintended fault.

"I'm sorry, Fan. I know it's you who bears the burden. What possessed him to openly write of her affair with your father and the painter—"

"I believe he did it out of love. I believe he wanted the full truth and picture of the woman he loved. I'm the one that mother writes of suckling her breast. I'm far more embarrassed by that image of myself."

Mary Wollstonecraft was my mother, as simple as pride can state it. She was as free a thinker and writer as the age yet knew. She was as revolutionary as the events she witnessed, and as controversial. Her chief concern had been the raising of children and the importance of education, even for girls, for she believed that for women to have a chance of standing in the absence of the wealth of a benefactor in marriage, an education was essential for security and independence. She was free with her affections and her passions as well, and it was this which had brought her reputation to ruin, and the blame may be laid at my father's doorstep. Fanny played a small part, but more for her own embarrassment, as mother in her travels in Norway wrote of caring for her infant in a strange land, and freely spoke of breast-feeding as a good and natural means of rearing a child, not easily accepted, though hardly as scandalous as the revelation of her affairs.

"At the least, you have a memory. I only have her ghost." I said, allowing my mood to surface.

"Mary!" Fanny chided me.

"No. I accept it," I said, only half truthfully. "I only have her books for her company, which the dragon hides from view, probably in the potato cabinet."

We allowed ourselves a small laugh and Fanny kindly did not press that tender issue which she knew I carried with me, ever and always, that I had been the cause of my mother's death.

"Tell me about Scotland," Fanny brightened with encouragement. "If I am to be sent off, your adventures might give me hope."

Our mother's relatives in Dublin would open their arms to Fanny, and the dragon would prevail upon them when she felt too threatened by Godwin's dependence on her. For Fanny, travel was a punishment; I looked upon my journeys as my savior.

"Fanny, I counted myself so lucky to go," I said as I looked out the shop window on the narrow dirty street crowded by another row of shops on the other side, packed shoulder to shoulder, with just twenty feet of grimy air between either pavement walk. I thought of the sea air in my face and I held up my hand in front of the window, so the light of day might show through the bone and sinews and vessels of my hand. I flexed my fingers, marveling that the machinery of life worked at all, for it didn't when I set out from Skinner Street for the north lands.

"I was seasick the entire journey, Fan," I said, hearing the wonder in my own voice. "But my arm was much better. The feeling returned to my fingers, almost as if by the waving of a wand in a magician's performance."

As I stood there, I could recall the sensations as if living them again. My hand was no longer framed by a sooted window, but resting on the mast of a ship, tingled by tiny stings of salty ocean droplets, sprayed over the bow and caught in the wind blowing toward the moors of Yorkshire, with journey's end still days away in Dundee at the Firth of Tay on the Scottish coast.

Doctors had been unable to cure my failing body. My right side, from the base of my neck to my knee, or very nearly, had taken on a numbness following my thirteenth birthday. My entire arm had lain useless by my side for three months. In its weakness, it had been an alien thing. How often I had thought of cutting it off, and replacing it with another, a body part which would bend to my will rather than its own.

I had been poked and prodded and fed the most vile of remedies, yet nothing seemed to have an effect on me. Three separate physicians could name no cause of which they had knowledge to explain it, though one had suggested it had something to do with the onset of my monthly blood flow. In this condition I would rage against my step-mother, for I could find no-one else to blame. So, finding no name, nor nostrum for my ailment, it was decided to send me for air, with a correspondent friend of father's. Why he would be possessed to send his young daughter to the house of a man he had never met, and knew only for his admiring missives, I may not be able to explain, except that that was my father, but we had become family friends; they had visited London, and I them.

The Baxters of Dundee were not titled, nor of noble descent, but of very comfortable wealth gained through their interests in the manufacture of textiles, as well as some fishing interests. I had three delightful companions in the Baxter daughters. I shared a room in their large house with sufficient grounds to roam, and magnificent trees to hide behind, when I wished not to be found. The numbness of my arm did indeed vanish after a week at sea, without explanation, and did not return, except for a recurrent twinge through the rest of my life which appears in times of some distress, and cramps the fingers of my writing hand when employed too arduously without rest.

The Tay at Dundee was most grey of atmosphere and the air smelled of sea salt and creosote. The "Cottage" which is what the house of the Baxter's was called, was located along on the ferry road to the bay shore, within a walking stroll to the fishing docks and a factory of brick built nearby. It was a large house, first built as a dower estate for the Countess of Strathmore. It was acquired by the Baxters as their enterprises became established. The new machines they employed to make cloth at an unheard of rate in the place of hand weavers, I found of the utmost fascination. Steam wheels turned belts to an extraordinary arrangement of metallic armatures, which would send a shuttle flying like a bullet through a spider's web of threads and spindles in a cacophonous roar that would wake a sleeping giant from slumber below the earth. I could see in those machines and steam wheels a shift in our future we do not yet know.

I enjoyed my days of company with Christy and Isabel, the younger daughters of the Baxter clan. We would pretend to teas and dances with princes, though more their designs, chiefly Christy's, than mine, or compete in games of lawn croquet. Isabel and I would especially treat ourselves to experiments in drawing spirits of ancient legends to make themselves visible; experiments which would produce results only in our fervent fancy, although Isabel claimed to have seen at least one ghost. We would watch the ships heave in the port, laden with whale oil and great fish from the frigid depths of the north ocean, with gnarled sea captains regaling upon us tales of great mountains of ice floating on the sea, the polar lights and navigating by the sextant and the stars.

Yet, even more impressed on my memory was the hill country away from the busy port, of woodless mountains, strewn with stones and brambles with occasional dales of heather and thickets of yellow gorse, or whin, as the locals named it. I would walk alone, in my pelisse coat, stepping among the mossy boulders and scrags of nature for stretches at a time, hopelessly out of place in my city clothes. There, my imagination would take flight. I endeavored to collect paper and pencil to write from the Baxter study and began stories. My prose was of the most abject simplicity and I am sure may still never be equal to the books which surround me. I didn't make myself the heroine of my tales, following the admonition of my mother's theories. My experience of life is far too common-place and I could easily populate the hours with creations far more curious and fascinating than myself. I would hide behind a great elm on the estate for my solitude, with a small writing board to balance on my knees and escape to worlds of my own devise.

I looked to Fanny, standing among the stack of books, trapped in a world with no imagination. I picked up a volume and felt the binding against my palm, within it another world, while without, a dreary dust mite beam of sunlight filtered by a thickening city atmosphere.

"I began to write, Fan," I said, drawn from my reverie, "like my childhood favourites." I recognized the volume in my hand was one of them, *Gulliver's Travels*. "Adventures far away. And fantastic fantasies."

Fanny smiled warmly at my passion, in sympathy with my dreams. "Mary, in the land of the Lilliputs," she teased.

"He never got seasick. And he could comment on his society while teasing the imagination. Mr. Swift, not Gulliver," I had to correct myself, at risk of confusing author with character, a dangerous slide, all too common. The smile fell from Fanny's face. I thought I had insulted her in some manner.

"Fanny, help our customer. We are not a lending society," came the command from the enemy, standing behind me. "Mary," she said, addressing me without seeing my face, "if you will set that book in place, the binding might remain marketable. "

I set the book once again from whence it came, while Fanny went to help the customer with her children, who needed no assistance at all. I stopped her on the way, between the games and stationary and whispered, for I did not want to engage the devil, but felt a chasm between myself and my sister that needed to be breached for her sake, if not for mine, for it was a cloud in the room as heavy as a winter storm.

"Fanny, do you mind that I see Mr. Shelley? That he—sees me?"

Her answer was silence, an unspoken pain, but we both knew it had been taken from our choice. She continued to the woman and happy children, leaving a wake of unexpressed regret, but no recrimination, so as not to increase my guilt.

"*The human heart is nearest moral perfection, most alive, and yet most innocent, aspiring to good, without a knowledge of evil*" could be said of my sister Fanny. That she could take her own life, but two years from this moment, is my most dreadful penitence.

~~~

CHAPTER THREE

St Pancras

The city gives way to the English country, not yet swallowed, where the New Road follows the edge of the fields in Somers Town, and joins with a fence which separates the wilds from the church yard of Old St Pancras. It was here I grew up, able to walk from our house, one of joined apartments in the Polygon on Clarenden Square, past the market square and across the road into the woodland groves and wild grass to the Regent's Canal. As I write this, advancing rail lines have made this vernal groveland their terminus, with commerce and industry forming to serve them, and it is no longer at all what I knew, but it was here I would arrange to secretly meet Shelley, in the old neighborhood of my fond memories, where we could stroll together unobserved by our present acquaintances.

Shelley was devoted to walks and afraid now to show his face at our door uninvited too often to arouse father's ire, when he did not hold a bank draught in his hand. He would join me from the canal, walking at his pace through the overgrown wilds. I would bring some bread and a hand bag for some books to read. We would stroll together as friends, invariably ending our journey at the old church of St Pancras, with its heavy Norman tower rising above an ancient cemetery.

St Pancras was named for the fourteen year old Roman boy beheaded on the via Aurelia for refusing wealth and honors to deny his deity. I had a particular affinity for the saint as he was the patron of children and protector against cramps, which on sea voyages I had occasion to call upon. My affection for the location was not for its historic or religious value, but as the final resting place of *she* who drew upon my heart and gave me solace.

As Shelley and I walked and talked, in unrestrained reveries of subjects far and varied, our conversations were at once naïve of our situation, delving, enlightening and entirely inconsequential. Shelley would stoop over a bit as he walked, so as to reduce his height over mine, and restrain his regular energetic gait to a tandem pace. The fields were in full flush of spring sunshine and bloom. Shelley stopped to smell a blossom.

"I like flowers. But don't ask me to name them," he said, without the slightest prejudice against nature, "*Beauty, bright sails upon the breeze.*"

He spoke of his youth, with many hours spent in nature, walking across distances and scrambling in the thickets. He hunted and fished a great deal as a boy, claiming he was a good shot, though not offering to prove it.

"The city has robbed me," he complained with a simple sigh.

"I miss the country," I answered as one intending to match the tone of a companion. "When we lived here, I could explore to my heart's content. The printing venture caused us to move to the bookseller's district. My stepmother's cause. I was so much happier when my father was content to only write."

Shelley astutely detected the thorn nesting under my skin, "Do you blame Mrs. Godwin?"

"For dragging father into business when he has no mind for it?"

"More than that."

"I cannot think of her without a feeling like disgust." I admitted it in honest revelation. "How she treats sweet Fanny like a servant rather than child. Then, she and my father complain that she is not industrious. She is so bright of mind, yet, when Claire and Charles are tutored in French and Greek, she barely is offered letters. Father could not survive without her correspondence on his behalf, yet she is no more than a slave. When the one thing our mother supported most was the education of women, her own is left lacking because she is blamed for scandal."

Shelley politely waited for my heat to cool a little.

"I'm sorry, I didn't intend to drag you into our family drama."

Shelley smiled. "I'm afraid I am in the cast already."

His smile was infectious to me and took me away for a moment from the fleeting thoughts of that principal tragedy of my family in which we played our roles. In his grief (for that is the only way I can hope to explain it) upon her death, my father wrote a detailed biography of my mother in which he revealed in stark directness, as if examining a history as public and far removed from personal connection as a fallen monarch, private details of both his life with her and of two of her love affairs before him. When published, this biography produced not the intended reverence for one so loved, lost, but rather scandal and disreputable notoriety.

We came upon a small pond where a stream which flowed toward the canal gathered in an impression in the uneven ground. Shelley paused for a moment, searching in his pockets to find some scraps of paper. The paper I could see had fragments of verse scribbled upon them, but without care for what they might contain, he tore them into squares and folded them into a little boats, kneeling down to float them on the water. He stood again and watched as the little airy crafts of white bobbed on the ripples.

"You don't seem to lack," he finally said, I think referring to my own education. This caused me to warm, allowing myself a little pride.

"I'm more insistent. I am denied at peril, when I am at strength."

Father had seen to my tutorage despite Clairmont's complaints of the cost, bolstered by my willful demands and my mother's arguments. And my appetite for reading could not be denied, though she would peeve at the appearance of a volume in my hands, and would cause the most vociferous of unpleasant scenes between us.

Shelley bent to send more boats, blowing on them. After an effort, he required taking a hard breath as if a struggle, and arose from the water's edge to observe his handiwork of miniature sail craft. As he stood beside me, I could not help to think that to me, Shelley was like breathing. He cared little for petty opinions. He admired my mother's works and seemed to relish doing battle with the commonplace. We walked further and he was drawn to think of his own past.

"I had an exceeding interest in chemistry when I was young," he said. "I always had bottles of noxious substances about at school. I accidentally swallowed some. I think it had arsenic in it, though I can't prove it. It still affects me. I think I might die from it, someday. Maybe soon."

"I hope not, at least until our walk is done," I joked with only half humour. Shelley had a streak of morbid expectation, as if he knew his life was proscribed to be tragically short, but the cause he speculated was not to be his fate.

"My interest in chemistry is more philosophical, now."

"You said you shocked your schoolmates at Oxford?" I slipped my arm into his, continuing our casual outlook.

"Volta's battery pile," he explained with a sparkle in his eye. "I had a device with a crank passing metal across points, which would capture an electrical charge in a jar of acid with copper and zinc. I found it infinitely fascinating. I believe electricity might one day rid cities of poverty." It was a continuing theme of his.

"Yes, your Utopia— What did you mean by *free love* in *Queen Mab*? I think I understand, but can you explain it?"

"Eternal matrimony for the sake of society and not for the sake of love is not a natural state. I think it's rather self-evident."

"Do you love your wife?" I asked, with I admit a curiosity beyond the intellectual. He seemed to ponder and weigh the question, and my intent in posing it, I suspect.

"The question is – did she ever love me? Or only my money. But that is a general question wherever matrimony is contemplated, is that not true?" His answer held a forthrightness cloaked in the abstract I came to expect from him. "That was my father's view, anyway. She thought it perfectly natural to turn her affection on my friend, Hogg, so why shouldn't I believe it to be natural, that it is the heart which chooses? And not the sermon, nor the dictations of fortune. And she possesses neither intellectual curiosity, nor the least sentient instinct. Most of our conversations are dull and domestic."

We arrived at the gate to the Old St Pancras Churchyard and paused there. A breeze arose, tousling the leaves of the trees and I thought I heard a baby's cry on the wind, the plaintive gasp of breath of an infant entering the world. Yet, I knew it was in my own mind, for I had heard it before. A ghost of my own self. A harbinger and a judge. The picture would not leave my mind; a beautiful woman in dim candlelight lay in a bed of soiled linen, her bare knees spread as the figure of a nurse bent over her, screaming in tortured agony as she pushed the creature from her womb, until the voice of a new life replaced that of the effort to bring it forth. The image was of my mother, and the infant, myself. She died just ten days after my birth, having never left the same bed.

We walked together to her grave and marker. A single stone of plain granite, on which my father had ordered to be etched:

MARY WOLLSTONECRAFT-GODWIN
AUTHOR OF A VINDICATION OF THE RIGHTS
OF WOMEN
27 April 1759 - 10 September 1797

"Do you believe in the absence of God?" I asked Shelley, though I was familiar with his public reputation on the subject. He and a school friend, Thomas Hogg, who would later become familiar to me, had published a treatise on the subject of *Atheism* while at Oxford, which had the effect of requiring his exit from that school, and his separation from the affections of his father.

"I have argued the case. My printed views on atheism got me expulsed from Oxford, along with Hogg. And my position has put me at a distance from my fortune. But belief in the absence of God requires a faith in my own reasoning I may not feel confident to claim. It is the paradox I argue, that a God can be all loving, all powerful and omniscient, while at the same time demanding, petulant and contradictory. I was such as a child, yet no-one asked my forgiveness. I do subscribe to death as a boundary, beyond which there is something better than the world we have made for ourselves. But ask God how he made the worm, he will not tell you."

"But you published anonymously."

"Anonymity is futile at this point. I am too well known by my opinions, and too intent that they should be known to pretend to it. Though, for my family's sake, I attempt at least the simulation of not printing my name."

"Can you reconcile with your father?"

"My views on deity, he can subsume. It's my views of his society, he cannot abide. I wanted to donate a portion of the wealth to come to me to assist the disadvantaged. My family feels it is a waste of money to attempt a balance of the scales—based on your father's ideas of political justice. And now, your father depends upon me."

We were standing at the grave. I pruned the grass around the marker and stone paving. Shelley spread a cloth so that we might sit on the dewy grass. He stretched out his long legs, looking opposite to me, resting on his elbow and placing his tall hat on the coping of the stone. I removed two books from my bag, each with a ribbon marker where we had stopped. I tore some bread from a loaf I had brought and offered it to Shelley. I did not eat, for my sustenance would be in my mother's words, for they were all I had of her, and they filled me. I opened *Vindication* and read to Shelley from the marker ribbon. And he listened. This was our ritual.

Our casual picnics at St Pancras had been enough to satisfy our mutual curiosity for several weeks into June of 1814, when far away events we thought of little relationship or connection to us personally, would have the most profound effect on our intimate lives. Shelley felt so compelled as to make an appearance at Skinner Street, with no advance notice, though the enemy lay in wait, ever on vigil.

It was about four in the afternoon when Shelley entered the shop, through the front door as any random customer might, and started through to the stairs to the residence above. My step-mother, Mary Jane, appeared from the alcove, as if by entrance from a hidden hatch from the netherworld and obstructed his passage. She stood with hands on her broad hips, weaving from side to side to block his egress, alike a harbour buoy blocking a shallows. She eyed him as if having caught a thief.

"May I speak to you, sir?"

Shelley waited in uncomfortable impatience, with one eye on the stairs beyond her solid frame.

"I wanted to inform you, I have sent Fanny to her relatives—in Ireland. If you follow her there, I shall hire a prosecutor." She was quite in earnest, and he tried to contain a sudden jolt of mirth at her general level of awareness and currency.

"Then, I will tell you, Madame— I have no intention of going to Ireland. I have been there."

"Do you mean to say you have no designs on her?" she demanded. "Your constant visits are disinterested?"

"I have found Miss Imlay charming. But I am not, and have never been, in pursuit of her affections."

"Then, you will assure me my daughters are safe."

Shelley bristled, "As long as my purse seems to be the source of their welfare?"

She paused with no answer, moving to another concern, seeming to skip the principal entirely.

"My Jane is very impressionable, at an age she may take a sudden flight of attachment."

"Jane?" Shelley swallowed his desire to burst into a laugh. "Then, I assure you, she is completely safe."

He looked once again to the stairway to where I was waiting above, having seen him approach from the street. He measured the steps to reach the rail in his mind, to calculate the distance before capture, but changed his mind. He offered the guardian buoy a polite bow, and returned to the front door, stepping outside, and walking away.

The sun had dropped low as I hurried through the streets, anxious to reach the city boundary. As I approached the gate to the church, Shelley was there waiting for me. I had not bothered with the accessory of a picnic supply. He watched my approach from the fields path through the flowers. A flare from the sun catching an upper casement window caught my vision, so that I had to close my eyes for a moment, but when I opened them again, Shelley was standing before me, a look of expectant excitement, as if he had great news. He took my hands and I his, I ached for him to kiss me, and would willing have returned it. We stood for the longest time; we could have stood thus for an eternity, until he finally spoke.

"Napoléon has abdicated," he announced, as if it were the arrival of a letter.

"Yes?" I responded, curious as to its importance. I had certainly read that the Emperor of France had been defeated in a series of running encounters with the combined military forces of Austria, Prussia and Russia, with sundry other participants, including our own Royal Regiments, following a strategic loss at Leipzig nearly six months ago, and had failed to reach Paris from his palace in Fontainebleau. The broadsheets had had the stories of battle reportage in regular columns for weeks. It had been since the 13th of April that Bonaparte had ratified the Fontainebleau Treaty, agreeing to remove himself to an island called Elba in the Italian Sea.

"A Bourbon is to return to the throne as Louis le Eighteenth." He stepped a small distance from me to separate us from touching. I walked with him, only allowing my arm to lightly brush his, not daring to lock arms as we were used.

"Does this make you sad, or glad?"

"The revolution is a lost experiment. Napoléon made himself emperor and turned the ideals of freedom into a perpetual state of war. Now, monarchy is the again the final result."

"I understand your point," I said.

Shelley had been a supporter of the ideals of the French Revolution as a young man, but had observed those egalitarian notions of freedom from class fall prey to the puerile and vindictive elements of personal aggrandizement and spoils of chaos. Now, with the fall of empire, rule by heredity was to return, though tempered by a constitution. But why it occupied his thoughts at this moment, I could not quite grasp.

We reached Mary Wollstonecraft's gravestone and laid out our usual arrangement in the grass. But nothing was usual in our secret hearts, even though we maintained a present propriety. Shelley was writing in a book of convenient bound quarter sheets he kept with him. As I watched him, he peered at what he had scratched on the paper, cocking his head to the side, then scratched something out and added a variation.

"Do you have something on your mind?" I asked.

"I very much enjoyed Paris in my time there as a youth. I should like to see it again."

"I have not been. I have only seen our country." I offered in casual reaction, then, thought more deeply, recalling where I was. "My mother experienced the

Revolution. She lived there at the time. She witnessed the king's carriage on the way to his trial."

I stroked the cold stone of the marker, imagining the scene. "Faraway lands draw me. Lord Byron's descriptions of Harolde's pilgrimages thrill my imagination." I could not help a laugh, thinking of my younger step-sister.

"Jane, who now insists on being called Claire, moons incessantly on the handsome features of Mr. Byron's face and the curls of his hair. This, though she has never met him, or indeed seen him in person; she imagines his voice speaking in her ear in dulcet romantic tones."

I observed Shelley make a last mark in his note book, and seem satisfied. "What have you written? Of revolution, injustice, freedom?"

Shelley held his notes to catch the slanting orange rays of the sinking sun, and read for the first time, words which would fill schoolgirls' dreams. "*Nothing in the world is single. All things by a law divine in one spirit meet and mingle. Why not I with thine? See the mountains kiss high Heaven. And moonbeams kiss the sea. What are all these kissings worth. If thou kiss not me?*"

I sat as if frozen to the spot. Shelley put down his pad and slid himself close to me. He took the book from my hand and set it aside on the grass. He took me in his arms and kissed me. I was not safe. And I did not mind.

~~~

CHAPTER FOUR

Claire

It was late of July when our course was set. Shelley paced in hurried stride on Skinner Street. He seemed distracted and upset from my window vantage. He had sent a note to expect his coming, but it did not contain any clue as to his purpose. He paused across the street, looking at the facade of the book shop, trying to make up his mind. He reached into his coat to withdraw a small dark bottle. He took a drink of the bitter elixir, that same which held Coleridge in its thrall, but diluted to a twelve percent solution to reduce its deleterious effects. Pacing, he replaced the bottle. From another pocket he drew a small pistol of two barrels. Making his mind, he strode across Skinner Street.

Shelley pushed through the shop like one possessed with a mission, past the book displays, and past my step-mother, before she could intercede, left helpless at the foot of the stairs, as he climbed them, swallowing them two at a time

Shelley leapt from the stairs to the parlour as late day sunlight filtered through the windows draped with plain curtains. He anxiously opened a door and looked in a passage. Not finding what he was looking for, he stormed to another, flinging it open. It was a long hallway, dim in the middle with a muted daylight at the end. I was there at the end of it.

I ran down the corridor to Shelley, but he did not touch me. He paced in the parlour, deeply fraught with unease, pacing again around the chairs.

"Mary." He seemed to have difficulty finding further words. I was deeply affected by his obvious pain.

"What is it?" I asked.

He finally stopped his pacing for a moment to face me. "I have asked my wife to come to the city and informed her of my intention to separate." He fumbled in his breast pockets for the bottle of diluted laudanum. I saw that he held the pistol in his hand, for he needed it to uncork the stopper and take a draught. He began to pace to and fro again. I could not take my eyes from the pistol, but he did not even seem to recognize that it was in his grasp.

"Yet, though I promise to secure a sufficient income for her support, she pretends disinterest. I believed she would concur with the sense of this, but she has always been the puppet of her sister who craves more!" He paced further, "I have never loved her! And I am assured she has been unfaithful to me."

I reached out to him, trying to offer comfort from my own pain. "The thought of a wife indifferent, hard to you, false to you, is sacrilege. It is torture to me."

He halted once again, turning to me, advancing as far as the dark and cold oil lamp. He now took notice of the pistol, staring at it as if it were a phantom from another plane. "I have pledged myself to you. Though I am bound by legal ties, I hold myself morally free to offer myself to you if you would be mine. If I cannot be beside you, I will die. I will—" He looked again at the pistol, as if wondering in his own mind, what was it there for?

I had no care for the weapon, for I had known his moods now for some time. I took his hands in mine and reached to touch his face.

"You have my heart, and my hand. And sacred is the gift."

He kissed my fingers, desperately with the pistol held, but forgotten. I took it from him and placed it on the small table which gave my father's chair company, and we embraced. I knew the labyrinthine intrigue of his marriage was of a nature to present us with difficulties, but I was assured of the naturalness of our joining. I was sixteen and the world was suddenly entirely simple to me; we would be together. In spite of all the voices we knew would come against us, we resolved on a plan to be free.

Claire, for that is the due I shall give her if I am to claim my own will, sat upon on the edge of the bed in the room we shared since my return from Scotland. She had already dressed for sleep and rested in her nightgown, pondering herself in a hand mirror in the dim light of a candle upon the side table. I was turning in my mind whether it was safe to reveal our plan to her confidence. As I observed her she studied her own face, round and pretty without being undone by her cleverness, presented under a curled hair cascade of tawny chestnut. From her face, she would angle the mirror at her bosom, as if examining them through the vantage of another, turning the reflection first on one, then the other, comparing the advancing shape.

I interrupted her, sliding on the bed sheets next to her. "Claire," I began, but she turned to me with all forthright sincerity.

"Clara. I'm feeling very English today. Much more round, don't you think?"

I held my opinion, as I was accustomed to do when she was in such moods of self-consideration.

"Clara, can you hold a secret?" I asked directly.

"Oh, I don't think it's a secret at all," she answered with a similar directness. Then she continued with her own concern, "Do you think a young gentleman of noble means would find me alluring? Be honest."

"You wish me to be honest?"

Claire set the mirror down, thinking about the question, and deciding, "No. Not entirely. If you were honest, I might believe you. And then, on whom could I rely to tell me what I believe is true?"

I tried to hold my flush of irritation at her usual thrust of mind which I found to be maddening, as I had a favour to ask of her, and offered an answer which I thought might set her mood in a receptive vein.

"I believe many a young gentleman would find you alluring," I offered, stroking the curl of her hair in sisterly assurance, "and more so every day."

"See. Now, I don't know if I can believe you. You only tell me what you know I want to be told. But I should believe you, if I agree, shouldn't I?" She picked up her mirror again and held it at arm's length with its reflection toward us.

"Would you pretend to kiss me? Like a boy would. So, I may know how it might feel. And if you don't mind, I will call you "my Lord" and touch your hair?"

Imaginings of encounters with the mad, bad poet were once again dancing in her head. I tried to be patient, as I was reluctant to upset her. And I did not want to ruin the sensation my own lips had known.

"I don't think you'll have the satisfaction you hope for," I explained with reasoned patience. "It will feel nothing at all like it should."

"Everyone knows you see Shelley," she whispered in sudden conspiratorial confidence. "In secret. So it's not. Secret."

"My secret is a plan. May I confess it you?

"Of course. My solemn oath," she crossed her chest, now fully engaged in the conspiracy.

"Mr. Shelley has professed his love. He swears he will die, if he cannot be with me."

"I could imagine nothing less. He can be a dramatic sort of boy."

"We are resolved to escape. We are going to Paris. We would like you to accompany us."

I had no notion how she would receive the idea, but she seemed rather excited by it. "You want me to come to Paris? The three of us? Is this free love? Oh, I am very curious."

I took the mirror from her hand and set it aside. I had had some questions of my own in regard to the concept Shelley had expressed in a short stanza of *Queen Mab* regarding the nature of men and women which had pricked a hornets nest of both condemnation and approbation among critical thinkers and society at large, giving Shelley his most public notoriety, and surely excited the imagination of a fifteen year old girl with her current introspection.

"I think free love is more a theory," I said, trying to cut short further expectation, then, formed the logic of my own reasoning for including her in our plan.

"Two of us alone, would be subject of scandal, you see? But three young people travelling together—Well, that is a tour."

She grasped the idea at once, "Of course. A continental tour. We could be very fashionable. You and Shelley could write, and talk—about whatever it is you talk about. And I can visit dressmakers."

For our plan of escape to the continent to succeed, Claire's presence among us would provide a patina of respectability, and she could act as our interpreter. Although my French was functional enough for casual pleasantries, and indeed Shelley's, arcane, Claire's current study and fluency would be very helpful to us, and I felt a need to enlist her into our plot, lest we be compromised.

"So, Mrs. Wollstonecraft was right, education should not go to waste," she declared, once I had explained the plan.

"But this must remain between us, until Shelley can obtain some money from his sources." I begged her confidence and she nodded that she understood.

"Should you write to Fanny? She was so melancholy when she left for Dublin. She had such an affection for Mr. Shelley."

"I don't know what I could say. I fear I could only add to her unhappiness, whatever excuse I might make." I was reluctant to have Fanny know truly how far our relationship had advanced, for I knew it would cause her pain, and I had no desire to increase it, even though I was certain she would wish me well.

"She loves you, anyway. I'm sure of it." Claire assured me, as she could see my mind. For all the flights of her fancy, she had a quickness of mind and deeper understanding than outer appearances might suggest.

~~~

CHAPTER FIVE

Clairmont

Mrs. Clairmont was in a fury. I tried to stay far enough from her grasp by keeping a chair between us in the parlour. My father remained in his chair, stern and quietly angry, but unmoving. Shelley's intention for us to be together had been expressed in a letter from Shelley to my father, over which they had words. I have not proof of how they came to the knowledge of our immediate plan, but I suspected that my step-sister may have been unable to contain her enthusiasm, or perhaps she had confessed it to her brother, Charles, who in general was disinterested in our feminine affairs, but on better terms with his mother than us.

"You are sixteen. And he is married." Godwin stated the situation with a declarative directness, very unlike himself.

"He doesn't love her," I pleaded, on the edge of having my emotion escape my control and endeavoring to bring as much reason to bear on my arguments. "You yourself have advocated the abolition of marriage—that human beings may not expect to be devoted to one person for a lifetime."

He indeed had written in great detail on the fault of marriage as an economic construct of society, but seemed entirely disinterested in accepting his argument reflected back to him where his daughter was concerned. "I will cut you off from my love, if you persist in this," was his threat.

"Then, you cut yourself off from Shelley's money," I answered, with a sharpness I regretted as soon as it flew from me.

His response was painful even in its calmness. "I have objected to marriage, but as a matter of property, and the restriction of wealth and rights. But this is reputation, daughter. It brings the ostracism of one's friends and of the society in which we must thrive. I would not have you subjected to the same scorn I have allowed to cloud *her* memory."

I knew he was thinking of my mother and his biography, but I could only press on if I had any hope of persuading him. "Suddenly, you're the one to care what society thinks? You write of its evil."

"Words on a page, to my shame."

"You indulge her, William," spoke Mrs. Clairmont, in her usual tone of put-upon self-pity. "Always.

Allowing her to be influenced by the ideas of her mother."

"Whilst you cannot even be honest about your own parents!? Without my father's name, yours would be a mystery! And without his talent—," I stopped myself from further declaration. I wish I could have said more of what I felt, but I knew the arrow would bury deeper in my father than the intended target.

My step-mother had married my father in the fourth year following the decease of my own mother. She had been resident at the Polygon in Somers Town and had heard of his reputation as a writer and philosophical light of publishing circles. Her true name, as I now know, was Mary Jane Vial, though that as well may only be as far as discernible. She had claimed the name of Clairmont from a never-substantiated marriage to a business man from the Swiss canton of the Vaud, taking that name from a village near Morges where he may have been from. She already had a young son, Charles, by him or another. When she became present with my youngest brother, William, my father married her in a hasty ceremony at Shoreditch where she was registered as Mary Clairmont, and they held a second ceremony at St Mary's in White Chapel, where she was listed as Mary Jane Vial. These, however, were not her only names, as she had served a time in debtors' prison as having passed herself as a Mrs. St Julian, in the obtaining of loans under pretense. She had been rescued by an unnamed benefactor and had come to London from Bristol with Claire as an infant and her son, where she met my father in his grief and emptiness with his two daughters, and there persuaded him to marry and establish their printing business. She had always maintained to Claire that her father was Charles Gaulis of Clairmont, of a prominent Swiss family, whom she had met in Spain and had died of cholera in Germany. She did have familiarity with those languages, though the truth of her travels, as with any impression of her past, was cloaked in uncertainty.

"And you will drag your sister into this abyss?!" she shrieked.

"She will be our chaperone."

Mary Jane Godwin was incredulous in silence. Father held his broad forehead in his hand.

I continued my argument, "Perhaps an exposure to the customs of a wider world might cause her to be more serious of mind. Despite the schooling you have given her, in preference to children not your own. I speak mostly for Fan, as she is unable to face you, not myself."

"You, little Madame, have too much education for my liking."

I was at the point of clawing her eyes, but father reached to my hands, pulling me to his chair, but not rising from it.

"Blame me," he said. "I married to protect your name. A woman, with sentiments as pure and delicate, as ever inhabited a human heart!"

I knew he was speaking of the central aspect of our joined misery which he could only truly connect to me, for he comprehended the blame I placed on myself. One may read my father's biography of my mother for more intimate details than I have heart to relate here, but be it to say that following my entrance into the world from her womb, after a long and agonizing wait for what doctors had said was a breach, the placentia did not separate. While two doctors could not agree on a course of action and my mother's warmth seemed to return to her for a brief time, a shock of septicemia overtook her, and her last days were of juxtaposed shivers of icy cold and spasms of fever, with my father never leaving her bedside. They had met in heated argument at the house of a friend, and had loved in common vision of philosophy. My father had never intended to marry, as he had argued against that institution, but once I had made my presence known within her, he acquiesced to the custom to give me a name.

"Even as she lingered, wracked by her shivers," he said with tears, pressing my hands together, "every muscle of her body trembling; she was determined not to leave me. That day decided the fate of the object dearest to my heart that the universe contained. And its loss, the greatest anguish I have any conception of. I beg you, not add to it."

I stroked his hands in return, very near to altering that determination I had vowed, until the she-dragon spoke, like the scratching of fingertips on a slate.

"Would you give way to her? Godwin, would you have her ruin us? These whims of independence, influenced by her mother, reading incessantly of her who burdens our reputation, even now."

I turned to take what I had hoped was a last and soon forgotten recollection of her potato face, and stormed past her into the hall, leaving her to work what influences she might attempt on my father's heart.

I needed something with which to travel. Our means would be light and our clothing the barest of that needed for decency and comfort. I recalled a case I had seen in a storage room between our bedroom and

Fanny's, now vacant. I threw back the curtain, still in heat from the recent parental exchange, and rummaged among some stray unused furniture, covered by cloths. I found the small travelling case that had been the object of my search, but in uncovering it I saw revealed the corner of a painting frame among a group stacked on edge against the wall, behind a folded game table.

I lifted the edge of the linen in intense curiosity, for I recalled paintings once hung on the walls when I was small, but that had long ago vanished from view. Yet, here they were, hidden in secret, as if they might be two garish or colourful to compete with Mrs. Clairmont's taste for the dull, drab and practical. As I raised the cloth from the first and most visible, a wave of recognition and an intense sense of tingling anticipation welled from within, tingling my stomach and piercing my heart. It was indeed that image of my mother I recalled in fondness, but had lost. There, lying on its side, she fixed me with a warmth of gaze in white folds of a blouse. It was the portrait painted of her by a family friend, Mr. John Opie, posed while I was four months present within her. I stared at it, overcome by longing and loss, and mystery. It had been removed from view. Yet, I soon understood.

Behind the first frame was another canvas, of similar proportion, also hidden away from observance. I tilted it up so that I could view it, drawing the candle closer. There before me, was a winged devil of green scales crouched on the bed of a woman. She was draped across the sheet, her voluptuous nude shape only thinly concealed by a sheer white dressing gown as if dreaming of ravishment, while a white horse of blazing eyes peered through the darkened window in animal lust. I instantly recognized the imagery of that now infamously known painting by Mr. Fuseli, called with simple effect *Nightmare*. I knew from my father's biography that Mr. Fuseli, a Swiss of Italian extraction, had been an acquaintance of my mother's, and the object of her intense affections, one of the affairs which caused so much storm of objection. But here was a version of that painting, which he had reproduced for several eager patrons willing to pay, which presented as a model that same likeness as in her portrait. There, among the dust of unwanted furniture and household discard, was that soul of so much passion and life, thrust away as refuse. From that moment, I resolved with renewed determination that once departed, I would never return again to set foot within that house.

~~~

CHAPTER SIX

Paris

My stomach took extreme exception to the jostling of the coach as it rattled and jounced along the oft traversed road to Dover, marked by the deep wheel tracks of previous conveyances. Claire and I had only pretended to slumber the night before, taking to bed in our usual manner as not to arouse alarm. We had escaped Skinner Street by way of the rear packing door to meet Shelley at our prearranged rendezvous. The dawn had broken through a layer of muted mist and we could tell we neared the coastal barrier by the exposure of the white chalk which broke through the green hillocks. Our pace was heightened as Shelley had induced the coachman with an additional sum to ensure an advance upon his usual schedule, as we were certain the alarm had been raised and a constable set upon our heels.

The port of Dover, within view at that great castle upon the hill vantage, was a bustling tangle of fishing craft upended upon the shore, having already returned from their effort, and lateen sails bobbing in the waves. Claire and I stayed with the coach, remaining with my small travelling case and a portmanteau, while Shelley searched among the docks for a craft to engage for a private passage across the waters. As we very much wished to cross the channel with all possible speed, we would not wait for the packet ship, but resolved to make the passage that same evening.

It was the 28th of July, 1814 and the heat of the day had increased with every increment of the sun's advance. If it were not for the sea air the heat might have overtaken me. Yet, beyond the temperature, the thrill of our escape and the apprehension that Shelley could find himself imprisoned should our pursuers catch upon us, was more than sufficient to treat me to a persistent nauseum. With some exertion, Shelley found a small boat with a willing crew to hire for our crossing, the seamen promising us a smooth voyage of two hours.

The sea began with a calm smoothness so that I was lulled into ease enough to withdraw from my case the paper journal I had taken from the book shop displays in preparation for travel. I began to write of our escape in the darkness and the unintended noise we had made which would have raised the suspicion of our intent, and of the haste of our departure, but upon consideration of the legal effect such revelations might have upon Shelley's freedom, I lined out that detail and began again with a simpler description of the facts of our journey; I would continue thus as I kept detail, reluctant to express too intense a feeling for what it might reveal.

The evening was most beautiful; there was but little wind, and the sails flapped in the flagging breeze. The moon rose and night came on, and with the night, a slow, heavy swell, and a fresh breeze which soon produced a sea so violent as to toss the boat very much. I was then dreadfully seasick, and as is usually my custom when thus affected, I slept during the greater part of the night, awaking only from time to time to ask where we were, and to receive the dismal answer each time, "Not quite halfway."

The wind was violent and contrary. If we could not reach Calais, the sailors had proposed making for Boulogne. They had promised only two hours sail from shore, yet hour after hour passed, and we were still far distant, when the moon sunk in the red and stormy horizon, and the fast-flashing lightning became pale in the breaking day.

We were proceeding slowly against the wind, when suddenly a thunder squall struck the sail, and the waves rushed into the boat. I was afraid we might all drown as reward for our presumption. Even the sailors acknowledged that our situation was perilous, but they succeeded in reefing the sail; the wind was now changed, and we drove before the gale directly to Calais. Shelley rested my head upon his knees, cushioned by a sail cloth.

As we entered the harbour, I awoke from a comfortless sleep and saw the sunrise, red and cloudless over the pier. The sailors cleaved the vessel to the pier which jutted out over the wide flat sand of the Calais shore. The sailors unloaded our portmanteau and we walked across the sand in our travelling clothes toward the boardwalk and the port hotel. Shelley slipped his arm into mine and supported me; I was exhausted with sickness and fatigue. My step-sister, in deference to her character and constitution, was ebullient with excitement.

The boardwalk in front of the hotel was busy with characters of all walks, in activity bustling around us. I heard for the first time the confused buzz of voices speaking a different language from that I had been accustomed, and saw a form of costume very unlike that worn on the opposite side of the channel; the women with high caps and short jackets; men with earrings. Ladies walked about with high bonnets or coiffures lodged on the top of the head, the hair dragged up underneath, without any stray curls to decorate the temples or cheeks. Claire and I marveled at their fashion. Claire tried to imitate the walk of the women who passed, presuming to take a lesson in the native style for her reference.

There is, however, something very pleasing in the appearance of the people of Calais. A reflection might occur that when Edward III took the city in the medieval age, he turned out the old inhabitants, and peopled it almost entirely with our own countrymen. But the manners are not English. We remained during that day and the greater part of the next at Calais. We had been obliged to leave our boxes the night before at the English custom-house, and it was arranged that they should go by the packet of the following day, which, detained by contrary wind, did not arrive until night.

Shelley and I left Claire at the hotel to take a walk among the fortifications on the outside of the town. The old walls of stone with specks of moss and lichens clinging to the pits and crevasses bordered wide fields where hay was making. The aspect of the country was rural and pleasant. Shelley drew me into a corner of a field; the grass rising well above our waists, enough to conceal us from eyes which might be observant. We lain in the grass, making a small bower of enough space for our enjoyment, separated at last from that stricture of approbation which in our own country would deter us from expression of our love. But barely had we begun to disentangle ourselves from our garments than we heard a voice, calling as if a ghost upon the breeze.

"*Monsieur!*" was the questioning cry. "*Madame?! Monsieur, vous ave un message d'urgence!*"

It was a porter from the hotel who had followed our path, but had lost our sight in the hay. I could not help a small laugh as Shelley rose above the grass to visible aspect. The messenger soon stood at the edge of our bower. He surely understood our intent, but said nothing of it. He held a folded paper. Shelley read it. The porter added in a discreet English, "A fat lady has come for you."

We returned with the porter to the hotel, where waiting for us was a sea captain in uniform, and with him, Mrs. Clairmont, in black travelling cloak and even blacker expression upon her countenance, standing beside Claire. The seaman was a Captain Davidson, commander of the packet ship, now arrived, standing tall and rigid, his buttons bright and wearing trimmed side-whiskers as we had seen upon other seamen at Dover, a fashion of the profession it seems. The captain stepped forward to address Shelley, gesturing for my attention to remain aside as if to have a private exchange, though I could clearly discern his strong Cornish accented voice.

"This woman says you have run away with her daughter," the Captain said, as if willing to reserve judgment.

"One daughter?" Shelley replied with an unwelcome amusement.

The Captain pointed to Claire, "If you have bound her by coercion, Sir, I must make a complaint with the France authority and hold your goods at custom."

I met Claire's eyes across the short but hopeless distance to determine her temperament. She seemed as equally curious as to mine, but remained wordless.

"She is free as she likes," answered Shelley. "I have no hold or bind on her."

I stepped forward to aid as I could. "She is my sister, Captain. She has come of her own free will."

The Captain looked from Shelley to me, then to my step-sister and back again. I could not tell what he was thinking, though I know his thoughts must have held many images, but as a commander in charge of lives upon stormy seas in risk of peril, he maintained a stolid and measured demeanor.

"The woman has brought proof documents of maternity. The girl is sixteen years. In France, she has majority. If she volunteers to step across the boundary of the customs district," he gestured along the boardwalk, "England can have no hold upon her."

"Let me speak to her," I pleaded.

The Captain held me away with a gesture of his hand. "Why don't we allow them to discuss it, Miss. If the matter is pressed, the local prefecture can be sent for."

I was restrained so from intervention while my step-mother took Claire with her into the hotel. The porter was dispatched with a message for the Calais district office of the Paris Administrative Police to come in haste.

An entire night was expensed at the hotel. Claire remained with her mother the long evening and once again in the morning. Shelley and I maintained our own rooms, separated from the discussion. The French authority had come all the way from Paris to adjudicate, but left again before resolution as the customs district held jurisdiction.

The packet ship was loading with passengers for the morning crossing when Claire and Mrs. Clairmont finally separated. Shelley and I could only observe from a distance. Claire kissed her mother, and walked from the loading ship toward us. Mrs. Clairmont lingered a moment longer, then boarded the gangway.

She would be gone from our lives, so I hoped. We had heard the harangue and complaint all night through the thin walls of the hotel, but Claire had held fast. She did not repeat to us the arguments of her mother, although I can conjure an approximation; but upon my asking her what she said in return, she was clear.

"She spoke with you all night," I said, to which she nodded with agreement, but offered no more. "What did you say?" I asked.

She smiled at me in that mode of self-amused distraction she could employ when it suited her. "I said, Goodbye."

On the 30th of July, about three in the afternoon, we left Calais, in a cabriolet drawn by three horses. To persons who had never before seen anything but a spruce English chaise, there was something irresistibly ludicrous in our equipage. A cabriolet is shaped somewhat like a post-chaise, except that it has only two wheels, and consequently there are no doors at the sides, while the front is let down to admit the passengers. The three horses were placed abreast, the tallest in the middle, and rendered more formidable by the addition of an unintelligible article of harness, resembling a pair of wooden wings fastened to his shoulders; the harnesses were of rope and the postilion, a queer, upright little fellow with a long pig-tail, cracked his whip. We clattered on, while an old forlorn shepherd with a cocked hat gazed on us as we passed.

The roads were excellent, but the heat was intense. We slept at Boulogne the first night. Upon setting out the next day, the first appearance that struck our English eyes was the want of enclosures, but fields flourishing with a plentiful harvest. Though French wine was a constant expectation, we observed no vines on this side of Paris. The weather still continued very hot, and travelling produced a very bad effect upon my health, and my companions were induced by this circumstance to hasten the journey as much as possible; accordingly we did not rest the following night, and the next day arrived in Paris about two.

There are no hotels in this city where you can reside as long or short a time as you please. We were obliged to engage apartments at a hotel for a week. They were dear, and not very pleasant. We followed a woman concierge up a flight of stairs, while a porter followed below with our portmanteau. The door was opened and we were bid to enter. As usual in France, the principal apartment was a bedchamber. There was another closet with a bed, and an anti-chamber, which we used as a sitting-room. Shelley dug in his purse but found little there. The concierge withdrew her hand unhappily and departed. Our money had been depleted. In our haste to depart from London, Shelley had not managed to procure enough funds for our entire adventure. He would send to friends for consideration, but in the meantime we might want to eat.

My sister and I lay our things on the bed. The cover was filthy. I hoped the sheets had more attention from the laundry. Shelley laid his traveling cloak on the narrow bed in the alcove. It appeared quite short, like the size for a child. We had not discussed our arrangements in advance; an oversight where Claire was concerned. We had been accustomed to sharing rooms, but it was now clear we could not afford as many individual quarters as we perhaps imagined.

"It's stifling," I said, as the heat seemed intensified in the confines of an upper apartment. Claire stepped to the window with the curtain drawn. She pushed the curtain aside and threw the sash open. Light cascaded into the room. She fumbled with the unfamiliar door latch, then opened the full length door, glazed in arched patterns, to reveal a narrow balcony; beyond was Paris. We could see along the Quai Des Tuileries with the river guarding one side and the gates and walls of the Louvre pressing on the other. At the end of our direct view was the Tuileries Palace, with its marvelous gardens.

"Paris!" Claire exclaimed, throwing her arms wide. A breeze came through the open window, refreshing in its hint of coolness, but piquantly aromatic in a not entirely pleasant way. I took a space beside Claire to look out, pulling the strings of my bodice to allow the air to enter and wiped sweat from inside my collar. I pointed to the vast Tuileries for Shelley, inquisitively.

"Is that where the new king will live?" I asked

"If the Russians have left any furniture," Shelley said as he joined us, three pressing against the balcony iron rail. He leaned to look over the city at an angle, to a hill rising in the distance, lying just beyond the city wall. He pointed to it for us, having studied a city map we had acquired with our last sous. "There is the Mount of the Martyrs, where Blücher intended to fire his cannon on the city after his victory."

The city's beauty was nearly untouched by the recent wars. Von Blücher, the Prussian general who had routed Napoléon at Leipzig, in command of the artillery at Mont Martre had intended to reduce Paris to paving stones from its heights, in punishment for the French Army's depredations in Silesia. He was persuaded otherwise and the city surrendered while the Emperor was never able to muster an advance further than his palace at Fontainebleau, 30 miles to the south.

"I hope the Russians left some bread," said Claire with more mundane needs in mind, "I'm starving."

"My purse is dry. We may perish in our shelter, unless we are thrown out." Shelley was worried, as he was the sole source of our well-being, and had begun to question his planning, or its absence.

"Maybe I can sing for our supper," Claire volunteered.

She calmly presented herself at the balcony, as if in a theater, and began to sing an Irish air in good voice. I had heard her sing before, and had complimented her pleasing tone in the presence of our family. Then, I noticed Shelley admiring her, as she looked quite pretty in the sunlight of the window, singing like a free Lark.

The heat was too oppressive in the mid-day for adventure to sights, but our need for funds was pressing and Shelley had a plan to obtain some finance. He obtained direction from the Concierge and we set out to a nearby district where shops of finer goods were to be found and there he sold his watch and its gold chain for eight napoleons. Claire and I waited for him a respectable distance, occupying ourselves with peering into the window of a shop for ladies bonnets and coiffure.

Claire brushed her hair away from her neck, sweeping it upward, "Should I pile my hair on top of my head? Is that French?"

I didn't have an opinion I wanted to share, but expressed the principal theory of our journey.

"You may do as you like. We are on our own."

"Without restrictions?"

"Other than manners and pleasant company, I suppose we are free."

She played with her hair in the widow reflection for what seemed a lifetime, until Shelley joined us, feeling the jangling gold coins in his hand. I knew the watch was very dear to him as an inheritance.

"I won't know the time, but we may dine. Eight napoleons for my birthright. The emperor is banished, but his face on gold may still furnish our living," he joked with a glimmer of sadness. I feared his mood might shift, but at least a meal would even us.

The sun had made its chariot journey across the heavens and about 9 o'clock we ventured along the boulevards to admire the Parisians on parade, and found our way to the Tuileries Gardens, formal in the French fashion; the trees cut into shapes, and without grass, while a fountain of waters sprouted from the mouths of golden fish and bathed voluptuous nude sea nymphs.

Shelley and I strolled, arm in arm, as the other couples around us, but Claire was possessed with mischief. She darted about, hiding behind the statues. When an aging Parisian couple with a heavy woman hopelessly out-of-fashion in heavily powdered face strolled past, Claire followed behind them, making a fun face and imitating the walk. She was, I must admit, making us laugh, to our great guilt, but then the pair noticed her shadow. When they turned to look, she pretended to be disinterested, stopping to admire and feign shock at a naked marble nymph.

After they had moved on, she joined us. "Do you suppose such sea creatures exist? Should I bare my bosom and swim in the fountain?" The notion of freedom seemed to have affected her mind.

"I, for one, would throw a coin," said Shelley.

"Should we, Mary?" she asked, daring me.

"It might be cooler in this climate. I wonder if nymphs catch cold in the deep of the sea." I teased in return, the idea of a swim, not unappealing. "And where do they learn the songs which lure sailors to their doom?"

"I might like to lure an audience." she mused with wistful hope. "Do you think someone might pay to hear my voice on a stage? I could perform a great tragedy, dying of poison, and then rise again to sing of my torment."

"I think you may be too soon for torment. You haven't had time for love,' Shelley offered.

"I think the torment comes first, then the dying," I said, adding some reason to the absurd.

Claire summed her thoughts, "Love—then torment—poison, sing a little, dying—then, a party!" Her entire concept of drama in a nutshell. "I hear they have wonderful and entirely scandalous parties after a theatre performance. Shelley, you have theatre friends." I knew where her mind was going.

Shelley was restrained, and ended the discussion, "I suppose torment and dying makes one very thirsty. I'm parched. And I'd still like to take in the processional arch, before we lose light."

Following the map, we discovered the Gate of St Denis, an arch of victory built by Louis XIV. It was a beautiful piece of sculpture, disfigured by the barbarism of the conquerors of France, who were not contented with retaking the spoils of Napoléon, but with impotent malice, destroyed the monuments of their own defeat. When I saw this gate, in its splendor I imagined the days of Roman greatness transported to Paris.

Shelley studied it with darker thoughts.

"Freedom and equality of men before a just order were smashed when the Russian Tsar rode through this gate on a chariot," he said almost as if lost in a reverie. Indeed, when Paris fell to the enemies of Napoléon, the revolution for brotherhood and equality was truly over. The Russian troops had marched in solid rank through this arch to place a new king on a resurrected throne; not for the war weary peoples of France, but the glory of the noble families who ruled in Vienna and Dresden, Berlin and St Petersburg.

Shelley was sinking into a darker place. He absorbed these histories into his thoughts and his expression of ideas when he wrote even of the most fantastical of fantasies; it was the progress of the human spirit which engaged him, and its dimming weighed on him. He reached once again into his pocket for the dark bottle.

We prepared for night. Shelley waited in the sitting room as we arranged our night shifts and got into the bed.

"*Entrez!*" Claire shouted when we were ready.

Shelley entered with a slight bow of his frame and examined the alcove bed. He removed his waistcoat and untied his shirt.

Claire peered over the sheets, but I pushed her face away. I must admit it was comical as Shelley tried to fit into a bed far too short for him. His feet thrust beyond the end, hitting against the alcove wall. He shifted his position and tried to curl his body to fit.

I couldn't help a comment at his expense, "A comfort too small for your mind to fit?"

"My intellect I can compact, it's my feet I cannot reduce," was his answer. He tried once again to twist himself, then, finally stood up again. He looked over toward us, in our bed. I looked at Claire, who seemed entirely amused, and recalled her question regarding the theory of our trip. We had no·one to report to, nor judge to answer to, save for whether I would choose to report in my journal. With Claire having no objection, I raised the cover to offer Shelley shelter with us. He accepted the invitation and came over to lay himself between us. It was a very snug fit in the bed. He laid his arm over me, with Claire behind him.

This comfortable arrangement lasted only until we began to fall asleep, when, with the slightest move, Claire was pushed to the edge and fell off, crashing to the floor. We all laughed at the mishap, and Claire climbed back into position, but as Shelley pressed against me to make room for Claire, I was forced to the precipice and tumbled off, crashing to the floor.

Our laughter returned and the full realization of the fault in our plans came into my mind. "This will take some practice," I said aloud.

Shelley gave in to the obvious and proposed his return to the other arrangement, "I shall make myself small enough for the other." But before he could rise, Claire stood and padded to the small bed in the alcove, in the most obvious, but freely interpreted theory of our relationships.

"No," she said, "This will suit me, just right." As she laid down and curled under the sheet, I thought of a story that a poet friend of father's and an acquaintance of Shelley's, Mr. Southey, had proposed for a collection of folk tales about three bears and a visitor who sought out a bed that was just right. At the time, it was a rather frightful tale in which the interloper was eaten and swallowed as a caution about venturing into other's lives. I mentioned this in passing to Mr. Southey some time later after he published his story, and the story when it appeared recently, had become of a curled haired innocent with golden locks, in the den where innocence was lost.

Claire watched us, studying us comforted in each other's arms, as I drifted to sleep.

Luminous clouds swirled above the graveyard markers of the Old Church at St Pancras as I ran among the stones, my bare feet in the grass and only dressed in a thin cotton night shift. A shadow swooped over me like the shade of a ghost, and even though I tried to run as fast as I was able, my legs would not carry me, as if the childish numbness of my arm had claimed them as well, when, in a blink, I had reached the stone of my mother's marker. I was held on the spot by some invisible force, as I traced my fingers over the letters *author* and I tried to speak, but my mouth was held, as if a governess restraining me as I tried to say the words, *Vindication of the Rights of Women*.

The shadow swooped over me and suddenly I was lying on the grave stone with the grass grown high around me. I was spread out on the cold stone. I was naked. I could feel eyes watching me from some unseen gallery above, and wondered why I had come, and why I had forgotten my clothes. The shadow above me formed into a winged creature of green scales. A white horse seemed to gallop around me in the tall grass. Suddenly, the arms of the dead shot up through the earth, decayed hands of rotting flesh in prison chains, grasped my arms and ankles. Dead corpses climbed from their graves, cracking their ancient stones and clawing from their tombs. I called for my mother, but my voice did not come, catching in my throat as if one of the dead were clutching it.

Lightning from the sky crackled and struck the dead. Then, Shelley was standing in half-undress at the end of the grave paving, like a tower between my legs, and he was turning the handle of his electrical generator, jolting me in a spark of excitement, and I was suddenly in a field of battery jars.

"*This book is sacred to me, and as no other creature shall ever look into it, I may write what I please*," I heard the voice as if coming from the sky, then the light of morning from the open window sash brought me to consciousness. The dream faded from me. I was wet and soaked with sweat. It was the heat.

I looked across the room to see Claire, sitting up in a chair in the morning light, her legs folded, with my own volume of *Queen Mab* in her lap. I should have been angry. She was reading from that private inscription I placed in it, never intended to be seen by any but myself. She must have found it in the case of books I had brought to while the time.

"*Yet what shall I write?*" she continued, revealing my secret thoughts. *"That I love the author beyond all powers of expression. Dearest love, we have promised to each other, although I may not be yours, I can never be another's. But I am thine, only thine—*"

"I found this among your books," she said with no apology or notice of my feelings. I looked around the apartment. Shelley was gone.

"There was some matter of a letter he needed to send. He said not to wake you."

I sat up and snatched the book from her, gently folding it and feeling its cover before placing it back into my bag, with a volume of Shakespeare and mother's *Vindication* and *Letters from Norway*.

"Those are my private thoughts," I chided.

"I wonder what it must be like to feel so. To feel so much love."

"You must find out for yourself one day," I spoke with some impatience, which I might myself regret.

"I must," she said, determined.

Taking the opportunity to advance my journal while Shelley had business, I found my paper and ink. I took up a position by the balcony window, to take advantage of the light on the page. I began to tell of our hotel and our sights visiting, and our sleeping arrangement. But then, on second consideration, I lined out portions and began again, heaving to my resolve to limit personal comment. I mentioned the Tuileries and the gate of St Denis, and I certainly couldn't leave out the Tsar, but I found there was little else I might allow. Perhaps other parts of our journey would be of more value to the casual reader, not interested in our small intimate lives, but of the strange wonders we would see. I looked out of the window at Paris, wondering how to describe it, and thought of the boulevards.

~~~

CHAPTER SEVEN

Neuilly

Shelley and I stood outside the gate of Chateau Neuilly. It was a sumptuous looking edifice of white alabaster and marble, only a half-century old, surrounded by a vast green park bordering the Seine River to the north of Paris. According to our guide, it had been built in 1751 by Louis XV as a reward to his Minster of War, the Compte d'Argenson, according to our guide; it had been a temporary residence of Talleyrand during the revolution, and had served as a ceremonial palace in the investiture of Napoléon I as King of Italy in 1805. It was beyond a very solid iron gate and a fence of spiked filigree, and currently unavailable to public visit. We had walked to see the sights and Claire stayed behind, as she had less interest in the historical. We had viewed the gargoyles of Notre Dame and the Hotel de Ville where Robespierre was shot and arrested in the Thermador of the great revolution's self-immolation.

It had taken some effort to reach Neuilly. The property had only recently been returned to the

Bourbons, who were once again to take the throne of France in the person of Louis XVIII three weeks hence, in what was intended as a constitutional monarchy as outlined in the Treaty of Versailles of 1814. It would soon become a palace estate of the Duke of Orleans, and as I write this, it has now been nearly completely destroyed in the return of revolution which swept across Europe, a scarce few months ago, rearranging the map of kingdoms and nations and allowing me to end my long held promise.

In July of 1814, we had not come as tourists for its historical position, nor its architectural value, nor its truly royal splendor.

"*In Xanadu did Kubla Khan a great pleasure dome decree—*" said Shelley as if grasping it from the air. I looked to see if he was reading it from the guide. He was not.

"What is that?"

"Something from Coleridge," he explained. "He recites it from time to time. It came to him in a dream, with the assistance of opium smoke. It is incomplete. I think he's afraid to reveal how it came to him."

"Why?" I asked, not thinking of Mr. Coleridge as especially shy of self-promotion.

"Why do any of us keep secrets? Fear of ridicule. Fear of being thought of as frivolous, or worse, banal.

If he publishes an unfinished poem, no matter how extraordinary parts of it may be, if he cannot complete it with the same resonance with which he started it, it may lead some to ask whether his work only has value under the influence of narcotic."

"Mr. Coleridge relies on his laudanum. Is it from the opium?" I asked, gently stepping on a tender ground, but deliberate, and grateful for the opportunity, for it contained a fear to me.

"He medicates himself. I find it soothing to my moods. I am rarely without it near," he admitted with a casualness which worried me.

"You know it has a history in my family. Mother tried to kill herself with it, over Mr. Imlay, Fanny's father. At least it was reported in my father's biographical account. Do you find you need it so much?"

"Only in extremis. I keep it with me, for when I feel agitated, but measure myself. I see Coleridge, and I do not want to find myself there. I do not have his dosage. But in any case, it's unlikely I shall live that long."

I said nothing else of the subject for the moment as we walked the neighborhood, the real interest of our tour, not the palace. It was in this neighborhood my mother had lived during the bloody revolution. She had been able from her small apartment to see the road where the carriage the Louis XVI rolled past crowds as he was transported to his trial, and the guillotine.

From Mary Wollstonecraft's Letters:

"About nine o'clock this morning, the king passed by my window, moving silently along (excepting now and then a few strokes on the drum, which rendered the stillness more awful) through empty streets, surrounded by the national guards, who, clustering round the carriage, seemed to deserve their name. The inhabitants flocked to their windows, but the casements were all shut, not a voice was heard, nor did I see anything like an insulting gesture.— For the first time since I entered France, I bowed to the majesty of the people, and respected the propriety of behaviour so perfectly in unison with my own feelings. I can scarcely tell you why, but an association of ideas made the tears flow insensibly from my eyes, when I saw Louis sitting, with more dignity than I expected from his character, in a hackney coach, going to meet death, where so many of his race have triumphed. My fancy instantly brought Louis XIV before me, entering the capital with all his pomp, after one of the victories most flattering to his pride, only to see the sunshine of prosperity overshadowed by the sublime gloom of

misery. I have been alone ever since; and, though my mind is calm, I cannot dismiss the lively images that have filled my imagination all the day."

Her reports from the revolution had brought her public notoriety, and it was while she lived here in Neuilly, that she met Gilbert Imlay. As an American, Imlay was allowed to traverse the city districts for his business. He had to pass a toll gate from Paris to Neuilly, to see mother. It was where they conceived my sister Fanny, and in his biography, father would to his ever-lasting regret call her "a barrier child".

"What possessed him to do that?!" I asked of Shelley, plaintive to understand the male mind, as if he might have a clue to the solving of my father. "And to write so openly as well of her love for Mr. Fuseli! His painting of her in his Nightmare is in our closet, hidden away. Along with Mr. Opie's portrait of her, while carrying the child who killed her."

"You cannot take the blame, Mary."

"If I don't blame myself," I explained as clearly as I could, "I might blame her. If I was not the cause of her leaving me alone, without a mother to love and guide me, then it would be she who abandoned me. Then, I would have nothing."

"And Mrs. Godwin?" he asked, knowing my mind better than I.

"To me, my mother is still Mrs. Godwin. The other I think of as Clairmont. She has even lied about that! She pretends her own daughter is legitimate, when she knows she is not, and yet she vilifies my mother?!"

"So many names— You and your sisters, each from a different father, so remarkably different in temperament, yet sharing a common beauty and mind. Have you always hated her so?"

"She came into our house when I was four," I said, trying to recall at least one warm image. "One has few memories of that age, but I remember being promised a new mother. I remember it as a cold December, but her arrival added no warmth." I saw an image of myself, as a child, holding out my arms to be held, but no arms to answer. I turned to Shelley with an aching sadness, "I recall only being aware that she was someone else's mother and not mine. And she has made no further effort to persuade me."

With the heat of the day, we arranged our time that we might remain out late and sleep through much of the morning. This would be the obverse of our later travels. Shelley, Claire and I spent much time at outdoor caffés, combining features of the English coffee house and tavern, a customary activity of social convention in that city, sipping from demitasse the thick and disgusting liquid, eating cake and watching a passing parade of Parisians and visitors like us from elsewhere, and striking up a conversation with those who might understand us, that we might practice our accents. We read from books to each other and ate more cake, as Marie Antoinette might have suggested, for it was all we could afford. I worried about Shelley's mood and was thankful the bitter concoction seemed to wean him from his own dark fluid.

In Paris, unlike London, modest women may sit alone, through much of the day, even in the midst of the men, unmolested and without comment, and even stroll about the city unaccompanied as they pleased. So encouraged were we by this freedom that Claire begged of me that we leave Shelley to peruse book stalls, which could easily engage him for hours, and that I go with her to visit shops. While I do not disclaim an interest in fashionable trends, and a curiosity at the differences in the French manner of woman's clothing from those of our English sensibility, the situation of our personal economy was very present in my mind; we had not a sous, nor farthing, to our purses, so that we might purchase even a ribbon for our hair. This did not concern my step-sister in the least; Claire had not the slightest compunction to worry shop assistants to sample and fit for trial every variety of color or shape which might catch her fancy, with not a thought to the absence of funds to purchase anything.

It was as a matter of fashion that drew Claire's attention late about our third night to a small street where Parisienne women of a certain style seemed to linger, in not the slightest definition of modesty, drawing the attention of men wandering past, who would circle and return as if beset by indecision, yet trying to achieve an appearance of indifference before choosing one to speak to, then departing again into shadowed alleys. Claire was most fascinated by this, studying as if she might incorporate the behaviour into a skit, until one of the women spied her observance and hissed at her in the most hideous of temperaments, as if we had fallen into a pit of the animal kingdom.

After remaining a week in Paris, Shelley received a response from a letter he had posted, which set us free from a kind of imprisonment there. It was a bank cheque from a friend which could be exchanged for French paper currency and hard coinage; a small remittance, but at least sufficient to take us to our intended goal. But how should we proceed? After rejecting many plans, we fixed on one eccentric enough, but which, from its romance, was very pleasing to us. In England, we could not have put it in action without sustaining continual insult. But in our present country, it should not invoke more than casual comment; the French are far more tolerant of the vagaries of their neighbours.

We had resolved to walk through France. But as neither I nor my sister could be supposed to walk as far as Shelley's energy, we determined to purchase an ass, to carry our portmanteau and one of us by turns. Early, therefore, on Monday, August 8th, Shelley and Claire went to the ass market, to purchase an ass.

Shelley and Claire strolled among the livestock in a stall market on the opposite side of the Seine River. There were asses and goats in makeshift wooden stalls held together by rope along the earthen riverside lane, strewn with hay and dung. Vendors sold firewood and old discards as well. Boys occasionally swept the dung soiled hay into the river where it floated toward the ancient spired cathedral. Claire had never seen an ass, nor a goat in living flesh. She was afraid to approach an animal.

"What is the matter with Jane?" Shelley asked about her name choice, while she was distracted by a tuft-chinned Billy trying to nibble at a bow on her dress.

"It's plain. It's common. It's my mother's name. I should not like anyone to confuse me with her."

"I doubt there is little danger in that." Shelley helped her shoo away the interested beast.

"You may call me Jane. That can be our secret," she said. Then, attempting poetic refrain, "From your fair lips, tumble oaths to my heart, Jane. Like that."

She leaned against him as she tried to avoid a ball of dung in the hay, almost falling over. He straightened her on her feet.

"If you want to try your hand at poetics, you need to learn meter."

"Must I?" she asked. "Rules and quatrain. Beat and emphasis. AABBAB— See, I'm not as foolish as everyone takes me for."

"I would never take you for foolish, my sweet child." He stopped his progress, staring at a round grey flank of muscle veined rump.

"What an ass!" he exclaimed. "That is an ass, if ever there was an ass!" He shouted gleefully, only to have the French sellers look at him like a madman. He enjoyed it.

"Could you compose a poem to an ass?" Claire challenged.

He paused to consider the task, then began in tempered rhythm, "If I loved an ass, I would— But remark upon the beauty, the shape, the hair, the cud. If ever there was an ass to love, that ass, my ass, would be. But love."

Jane giggled at her poem, "But love, an ass. A sonnet in AABAB by Percy Bysshe Shelley and Jane."

He had been laughing through it, too, and smiled at her. "And Jane. Well, not a sonnet, more in the manner of a roundelay, ABAAB."

Shelley negotiated with the livestock vendor for a less expensive animal, while Claire noticed her feet. She was standing in a fresh pile of dung. She surreptitiously raised her ankle to wipe her shoe on the pant leg of a man behind her, otherwise occupied examining some goats.

~~~

CHAPTER EIGHT

Nogent

The rest of the day was spent preparing for our departure, during which, Madame L'Hôte paid us a visit to dissuade us from our design. She represented to us that a large army of defeated French regiments had been recently disbanded.

"*Mais non!* No!" she argued in half-English and half-French, gesticulating. "Idle soldiers and officers roam the countryside. The ladies would be taken— *les dames seroient certainement enlevées!* Monsieur, you cannot—!" But we were proof against her arguments, and packing up a few necessaries, leaving the rest to go by the diligence, we departed in a small *fiacre* coach from the door of the hotel, with our little ass following.

At the city gate, with country stretching out beyond, we dismissed the *fiacre* at the barrier. It was dusk, and the ass seemed less than suited to his task, appearing to sink under the portmanteau, though it was small and light, when the carriage driver lifted it to lay across the wooden saddle cleats, appearing barely able to stand with the trunk. The creature brayed with complaint. Shelley and I tried to assist Claire to mount it, but both she and the animal seemed to dislike the idea, unable to stay on.

The ass seemed totally unable to bear even one of us, but we were merry enough and thought the leagues distance to Charenton short enough; we set out at dusk in the evening temperature. Claire walked ahead and started down the road into the fields. Shelley took the lead of the animal, his first attempt as an ass driver, and yanked it. He yanked it, again. Finally the stubborn beast decided it might be less distraction to walk than not, and followed him.

We arrived at Charenton about ten. It is prettily situated in a valley, through which the Seine flows, winding among banks variegated with trees. The lights of the late sky reflected on the flat flowing waters of the river as it flowed through wild shores under a bridge to the town. Claire rushed excitedly to the stone edge of the crossing, with the glow of a set sun behind the village of small houses in the distance.

On looking at this scene, Claire exclaimed, "Oh! This is beautiful enough! Let us live here." This was her exclamation on every new scene, and as each surpassed the one before, she cried, "Oh, I am glad we did not stay at Charenton, but let us live here." She was imagining a complete escape from our former lives. Shelley and I were less certain of what our future held.

Finding our little ass hopeless, we sold it at Charenton and bought a mule, for ten napoleons. Though, I soon longed for the temperament of our ass. I made an effort to mount the mule, but it was reluctant for a passenger, kicking its hind leg in violent manner. This caused some amusement with Claire, and I made a helpful suggestion in reference to her common refrain.

"If you can't contain yourself, perhaps you'd like to stay and live here." She remained silent.

We progressed on the road clad in black silk. I rode on the mule, which carried also our portmanteau. Shelley and Claire followed, bringing a small basket of provisions. The mule seemed to manage my weight, though it was not comfortable. At about one we arrived at Gros Bois, where we stopped for rest, and under the shade of trees, we ate our bread and fruit, and drank our wine, thinking of Don Quixote and Sancho.

The country through which we passed was highly cultivated, but uninteresting. We met several fellow travellers, but our mode, although novel, did not appear to excite any curiosity or remark. Our black silk added to the heat and I wondered if we might have made a better choice for our tour. We had not accounted for so much exertion and the unfamiliar climate. The mule, when sedated, seemed to manage my weight with our portmanteau.

We slept the night at Guignes, in the same room and beds in which Napoléon and some of his Generals had rested in the late war. The old woman of the place was highly gratified in having this little story to tell, and spoke in warm praise of the Empress Josephine and Marie Louise, who had at different times passed on that very road.

As we continued our route, Provins was the first place that struck us with interest. It was to be our stage of rest for the night. We approached it at sunset and after having gained the summit of a hill, the prospect of the town opened upon us as it lay in the valley below. A rocky hill rose abruptly on one side, on the top of which stood a ruined citadel with extensive walls and towers; lower down, but beyond, was the cathedral, and the whole aspect formed a scene for a painting. After having travelled for two days through a country perfectly without interest, it was a delicious relief for the eye to dwell again on some irregularities and beauty of the country. Our fare at Provins was coarse, and our beds uncomfortable, but the remembrance of this prospect made us contented and happy.

We dined at a small wooden table set for our use outside a small inn, above which rose the hilltop tower of a ruined castle, a shape rising to a point like a black crown of stone. While we picked through our bill of fare, the innkeeper brought us wine which had a pleasant flavour. Shelley inquired of him what the castle was called and whether it was resident with occupants. The simple fellow appeared confused a moment, then his visage brightened with some pride for the local feature of his village. Claire interpreted for us his unfamiliar words as best she could discern, learning: the fortress was abandoned and had previously belonged to the Counts of Champagne; it was called the Emperor's Tower, or Caesar's Tower, as it had been in use to collect taxes and guard the passage of the Seine for the descendants of the crown of Charlemagne; and there was no-one at home.

With much excitement to visit such a feature of the present landscape, we hurriedly finished our meal and climbed the tower; I admit unsteady from the wine. It was in a dreadful state of neglected disrepair, dark and hard to see as we scampered on the broken stone steps of the ruin, our youthful laughter echoing among the stones of incomplete chambers. I climbed carefully, cautious of my step, but Claire leapt with heedless abandon from stone to stone where the old stair had crumbled, with Shelley following behind her.

We arrived on the battlement at the summit of the tower, where a defensive stone rail was all that separated us from a steep precipice. The landscape below was cloaked in the shadows of a sunken sun, while a few dim lights shone among the thick and dark wooded plain, and a glow in the far distance rested on the horizon, separating earth from the vault of the sapphire sky.

Shelley recognized the import of the far off glimmer. "That must be Paris."

"Have we come so far?" Claire marveled in wonder.

"It is only the commencement of our adventure," he answered.

Claire reveled in what she expected was now a famous notoriety. "I shall never wish to go home again. We are pariahs to friends and the subject of delicious gossip to our class."

I knew she was closer to truth than she herself believed. The landscape below us seemed to represent a boundary between our former existence and what was our unknown adventure ahead.

"We should go down," I said, worried, "before it's too black to find our way."

When we turned to go, I heard a shriek of terror from Claire. She had taken a step on an unsteady stone. Shelley grasped her to restrain her from falling over the edge. She clung to him.

"You've let me have too much wine," she said, still holding him.

"You must be careful where you step."

As I watched them, I thought my sister might be performing a small drama of which I knew her capable, causing her rescue to seem more dramatic than necessary. She held onto Shelley with both of her hands, neither reaching for the steadier rail which would have prevented any real danger of falling below, nor bracing herself. Shelley took his hands from her waist as she steadied herself again on solid stonework.

We returned with temperate care downward through the stone cave with Claire's voice in bursts of soft laughter behind me, being assisted in guidance for her steps by Shelley, who could scarcely see well enough himself. This was an adventure I would chose not to include in my journal.

Departing from Provins, following the track which led through the dry moat surrounding the immense walls, we now approached scenes that reminded us of what we had nearly forgotten; that France had lately been the country in which extraordinary events had taken place.

We travelled through a landscape of fallow fields and ruined, burned farmhouses, until we approached the gates of a town that seemed in all presence to have been struck by a blast.

Nogent, a town we entered about noon the following day, had been entirely desolated by the Cossacks. Nothing could be more entire than the ruin they had spread as they advanced.

We walked with our mule in tow down a narrow village street, past cottages with smashed windows and burned roofs. Perhaps they remembered Moscow and the destruction of the Russian villages, but we were now in France, and the distress of the inhabitants, whose houses had been burned, their cattle killed, and all their wealth destroyed, has given a sting to my detestation of war, which none can feel who have not travelled through a country pillaged and wasted by this plague, which, in his pride, man inflicts upon his fellow. The houses had been reduced to heaps of white ruins, and the bridge across the river destroyed. We stopped at a cottage that appeared intact, or at least reconstituted enough to live in, and asked if we might purchase some milk. They had none to give. All their cows had been taken by the Russians and then the Prussians, returning to their own country.

Shelley stood in the middle of road with the rope of the mule only loosely in his hand, looking around, examining the devastation. This village of Nogent had been one of the principal objects of our journey. We stood beside him, unable to offer solace to his sadness.

"This is where Rousseau found inspiration," he said, turning from vantage of ruin to burnt timber tossed to piles. "This is where Abelard loved Heloise; where she was locked in her convent and writing her letters. This—" his shoulders seemed to lose all vitality, "is where Romance is born. This—devastation."

Rousseau's inspiration had been one of the passions which had engendered Shelley's desire to visit a far and unfamiliar land, and of mine, to behold with our own sensations that environment from which the human story evolves and from which that name which has been given to our inadequate efforts to give it form, Romantics, had come.

With the bridge destroyed, we quitted the main road soon after we had left Nogent, to strike across the country to Troyes, hoping that all our journey would not be thus presented with disappointment, yet we still passed once beautiful villages, destroyed; abandoned to insects, which feasted upon the ruined fields. About six in the evening we arrived at St. Aubin, a lovely village embosomed in trees, but on a nearer view we found the cottages roofless, the rafters black, and the walls dilapidated; only a few inhabitants remained. We asked here for milk in the countryside, but they also had none to give; all their cows were taken, or roasted for meat. We had still some leagues to travel that night, but we found that they were not post leagues, but the measurement of the inhabitants, and nearly double the distance. Notwithstanding the entreaties of the people, who eagerly desired us to stay all night, we continued our route to Trois Maisons, three long leagues farther, on an unfrequented road, and which in many places was hardly perceptible from the surrounding waste.

The road lay over a desert plain, and as night advanced we were often in danger of losing the track of wheels, which was our only guide to civilization. I walked hurriedly, peering into the dark shadows, wondering with dreadful anticipation if any of the soldiers of the dismissed regiments of the *Grand Armée* of which we had been warned, might be encamped in the forest. It was Claire's turn to ride the mule as Shelley tugged its lead.

"Mary, you must be careful or you'll twist an ankle." His caution was from behind my back. I was feeling an increasing annoyance that we had left so late as to be in danger of losing our way.

"It's growing dark," I shouted back toward them, reminding, "You heard the warning of that woman in Paris. There might be soldiers in the woods."

"Or beasts of some fantastic imagining?" He teased me, recalling some of the tales I had invented in my youthful attempts at writing in Scotland, I had revealed to him, and my dreams. "Wolves of eternal night, or bones of dead armies reaching for you?"

"She's afraid she may have a nightmare." Claire added to annoy me.

Shelley was amused, but I was not in the frame of mind for mirth.

"You're the one whose terrors are horrid, Jane!" I reminded her, both forgetting that promise to keep her romantic notions of identity, and mindful of the night horrors she had experienced since childhood. Where my dreams were fanciful and lucid, hers were sharp and devoid of description, but pierced her slumber with dreadful screams upon awakening; recreated in scenes she might perform in public, when it suited her need for attention.

"We are in a desolate foreign place," I reasoned, suppressing my own real fear of becoming lost. "With little money, nothing to eat, and a mule for our only company and protection. And you seem to have no care for our circumstance. We don't know our way, and how are we to find rest in the dark, if all the inhabitants are gone to bed!"

Shelley took pity on me, taking on a more serious demeanor. Claire took the more practical response.

"I am hungry," she declared.

Night closed in, and we soon lost all trace of the road, until a dim light indistinctly seen, seemed to indicate a village, or at least a household.

"Civilization! At last!" said Shelley with a satisfaction. He helped Claire down from the mule and she determined to secure our route to town.

"*Je parler avec les inhabitants—*" she declared and hurried with light step cracking on branches into the dark woods, before I could stop her.

"Claire—!" I called, hoping she would stop. "Jane!" when she would not, vanishing into the shadows. Then, in complete abandonment of my reason, "Clara!"

I looked to Shelley, wondering what to do. How could she be so impetuous? And what lay in wait in that dark and shadowy bramble between us and the light of a farmhouse, at least so I hoped it was. We waited. Then we waited a bit longer. No sound came from the direction she had gone.

"Should we go to see?" I asked Shelley in fear. I heard a crack of a branch, but could not tell from which direction it came. Was it Claire who would appear from the woods? Was it a soldier, hungry for more than scraps of food, or was it a beast? I could no longer tell the direction from which the sound had come, filled with dread.

"Is it soldiers? Should we find her? Where did she go?" I railed in excitement to Shelley, who seemed entirely less concerned than I. "If she is harmed. I have brought her here. I am at fault if she is hurt!"

Just then, a ripple of laughter drifted across the night breeze. It was Claire's voice. How could she be laughing when I was filled with such expectation of horror? Yet, through the threes she reappeared, in the same manner in which she had gone.

I was angry. "What if you had been taken?!"

"You needn't be an ogre," she responded, taking my worry for her not with the slightest care. "I was perfectly safe. I spoke to some farmers and they said there is an *auberge* ahead."

She started walking. I recovered my fright, but was still filled with imaginings of what might have happened to her.

"Is that all? What else did they say?

"That it wouldn't suit our tastes," was her last word.

The inn was more a sort of a barn, and having in some degree satisfied our hunger with a supper of milk and sour bread, we retired to rest in a wretched apartment, more a loft of narrow beds; it was nothing more that sheets spread upon straw on a raised platform. We viewed the accommodation with a rueful disappointment. The sheets were soiled and rumpled, of the most disgusting presentation.

"I hope these inhabitants at least wash themselves," I heard myself say.

"In the worst, we may gain some travelling guests," was Shelley's joke, in one of his more ebullient tempers, when his attitude could cause the opposite effect in me. We kept in our clothes, but sleep is seldom denied, except to the indolent and I slept soundly until the morning was considerably advanced, when I was awakened by the most raucous of scenes.

A high shrieking cry and a thumping of heavy movement of the floor of the room aroused me from a dream. Claire was running around the beds, with giggles of laughter while Shelley chased and tried to catch her, like children at play. I called to them to stop their antics, but they gave me no notice whatsoever. Claire dashed around me to hide behind the next bed platform. Shelley, to cut off her escape, leapt from bed to bed, but the unsteady wood frame toppled, and he was dumped to the floor. His laugh turned to a groan of pain.

I hurried to his side, worried at what damage he had done. He held his ankle in pain. "Shelley! What have you done? Have you hurt yourself?" I asked him with great care for his well-being.

"I have made a gambol—and lost," was his reply; but I did not feel the events so worthy of mirth and held back a temptation to damage him further.

"I don't think it's broken," he said, moving it with care, and a wince.

Claire stood by, regaining breath. I tried not to blame her too much.

"Help me stand," Shelley said, holding out his arms like a child.

We took him under the arms from either side and assisted him to rise. He pressed some weight on the foot. It was not broken and he could limp.

We were not able to set on our way till eleven o'clock as Shelley's injury hindered a rapid pace. He had hurt his ankle so considerably he was obliged all the following day to ride on our mule. I walked in the lead of our procession, desiring to look upon neither of my companions. Our progress was a difficult enough task without Shelley's antics in his moods of heightened jocularity adding complication. He called to me from the back of the mule in plaintive hope for my forgiveness, with offers to behave himself in the future; but for the full morning, I would not be mollified.

Nothing could be more barren and wretched than the track through which we now passed. The ground was chalky and uncovered even by grass, and where there had been any attempts made towards cultivation, the straggling ears of corn discovered more plainly the barren nature of the soil. Thousands of insects, which were of the same white colour as the road, infested our path. The sky was cloudless, and the sun darted its rays upon us, reflected back by the earth, until I nearly fainted under the heat. A village appeared at a distance, cheering us with a prospect of rest. It gave us new strength to proceed; but it was a wretched place, and afforded us but little relief. My earlier arguments with my companions now seemed inconsequential.

The village had been once large and populous, but now the houses were roofless, and in ruins that lay scattered about the gardens covered with the white dust of the torn cottages, black burnt beams, and the squalid looks of the inhabitants, presented in every direction the melancholy aspect of desolation. One house, a cabaret, alone remained; we were here offered plenty of milk, stinking bacon, sour bread, and a few vegetables, which we were to dress for ourselves.

As we prepared our dinner in a place so filthy that the sight of it alone was sufficient to destroy our appetite, the people of the village collected around us, squalid with dirt, their countenances expressing everything that is brutal in the human species. They seemed indeed entirely detached from the rest of the world, and ignorant of all that was passing in it. There is much less communication between the various towns of France than in England. The use of passports may easily account for this; and these people did not know that Napoléon was deposed. When we asked why they did not rebuild their cottages, they replied that they were afraid the Cossacks would destroy them again upon their return. Echemine was the name of this village and in every respect the most sad and disgusting place I have ever met with.

Two leagues beyond, on the same road, we came to the village of Pavilion, near, yet so unlike Echemine, that we might have fancied ourselves in another quarter of the globe. Here everything denoted cleanliness and hospitality. Many of the cottages were destroyed, but the inhabitants were employed in repairing them. What could occasion so great a difference, whether guidance by local authority or the influence of some positive spirit, we could not determine.

Still our road lay over this track of uncultivated country, and our eyes were fatigued by observing nothing but a white expanse of ground, where no bramble or stunted shrub adorned its barrenness. Towards evening we reached a small plantation of vines; it appeared like one of those islands of verdure that are met with in the sands of Libya, but the grapes were not yet ripe. Shelley was totally incapable of walking, and Claire and I were very tired with painful sores upon our feet before we arrived at Troyes.

~~~

CHAPTER NINE

Troyes

The city of Troyes (pronounced by locals with a guttural abandonment of vowels), the largest town of the Champagne region is formed of a collection of medieval houses of dark timber and coloured plaster in narrow streets. We led the mule with Shelley astride it down one of the streets. His legs, thrust from either side nearly touched the walls which bounded the avenue. We had been directed to this quarter from an inquiry with a helpful resident who had a familiarity with travellers and knowledge of his own city.

We came to the object of that direction we had been given; an inn which appeared to have been present since the days of medieval pilgrims. A painted sign declared it grandly to be the Auberge of the Counts of Champagne, but from its outer aspect it seemed unlikely to have ever received such noble patronage. Shelley reminded us that we might be as knights of old arriving on a steed to seek shelter

"An accommodation surely fit for counts and princes," he joked. Then, as we assisted his dismount from our poor mule, he cried out in agony and collapsed to the road. An inhabitant from within emerged to assist us in releasing our portmanteau from the mule as Shelley was hopeless. While Shelley's sprain and our shoes rendered further pedestrianism impossible, we resolved that despite the cost, the following day we must purchase a conveyance, so that all may ride.

In the morning, Shelley's ankle was improved, yet still tender. Claire remained asleep until late as we had allowed a day while Shelley and I intended to visit the cathedral of the city. We rested in an outdoor courtyard of the inn. The innkeeper had promised us a large breakfast, which seemed to consist mostly of two kinds of bread and some sour butter. I had a place where I could rest against a bench out of the morning sunlight which reflected brightly off the plaster of the walls, to write in my journal. Shelley was opposite to me, with his leg stretched out, resting his foot as he made some marks on a loose sheet of paper. He must have presumed I was not observing, so lost in my writing, to not see him reach for his pocket to take a drink from his laudanum. His previous jocular mood had turned to melancholy, as he was distressed at his injuring himself. I made no mention of it and endeavoured to appear as if I had not seen. I was happy, at least, that he was distracting himself with his own expression, focused so intently; I did not know that what he was writing was a letter to his wife. He glanced over to me as he waved the ink dry and folded it. He started to rise, but winced when he put weight on his foot. He sat down once again with a grunt. I made casual mention of the folded paper in his hand.

"Do you write something? Have you started a story? A poem?" I asked, in all innocence. "May I see?"

Shelley looked at the paper in his hand with an expression that he might be reluctant to explain it, as if to one below his sophistication. Then, instead, he held it out to me.

As I read the letter, I could feel my face flush. In it, he urged Harriet to come to join us in Switzerland, where he, "*who would remain her best and most disinterested friend, would procure for her some retreat among the mountains*". He told her in simple unadorned detail of some of our journey.

"How can you send this?" I demanded.

"I owe her my good will. She faces the public scorn of our parting. She would be safe here."

"How do you know she won't use this against you?! She could publish this to bring us down!" My most urgent concern was that his revelation of our progress could be a weapon in the hands of enemies, but then another more stinging thought came to me.

"Do you still want to be near her?" I asked him.

"Do I say so in the letter?"

"What we say and don't say in our writings can be mistaken. Or read between words."

He pushed himself up despite the pain and leaned toward me, gesturing to my own journal with lines blackened through it, where I had chosen what I might be unwilling to reveal.

"You choose your words carefully."

"I am not as free a soul as you." I welled with some emotion, recalling all too dearly that a forthright personal revelation may have deep consequences. "My father was too honest in his in homage to whom he loved, and we all pay for it. I am more careful. I must be."

Shelley understood me. I begged him not to send his letter. He again folded the paper in his hand and hobbled toward the entrance to the inn.

"I have to sell a mule," he said. "I'll take Jane for support. Stay and finish your entry."

"You seem to take pleasure in my sister's company."

"She has a wit to her mind. And a sprite naiveté that amuses me." He said it without a hint of guile.

"I'm glad." I said, and he left me to my journal. I still do not know to this day whether he sent that letter to his wife, but I did have later an account from him of his adventure with Claire in selling our mule.

Claire lent Shelley support with her arm, as he stepped gingerly on his foot, pulling the mule with its saddle empty toward the market square of the town. It was on another narrow street which turned with angles, so that no view could be had of its entire length. It was in one of these angled segments where they hesitated for Shelley to rest his foot. They waited as two city residents passed them, taking what was surely a common route to their market, but made no remark to the two mismatched young foreigners, holding the rein of a mule.

The mule also took the occasion of rest to relieve himself of a healthy load of his previous meals onto the stone paving, amid the other random bits of evidence of animals passing to market. Claire waited until the residents passed from view and faced Shelley.

"Will you kiss me?"

Shelley was surprised by the request. "Now? Wouldn't you rather wait until he pisses?" But Claire was inured to irony and in earnest.

"I want to know what it is like. I have never been kissed. I have imagined it in great detail, but have nothing to compare to."

Shelley did think her pretty, and had not been without notice that she might be ready for it and worthy of it. He had by now kissed two of my family and the third held some curiosity for him, though if it was his choice and he free to make it, might have selected a more idyllic environment for the experiment. He took her squarely in his hands by the shoulders. She closed her eyes.

"The firsts that memories are made of," he joked, and kissed her.

"Might we do it again?"

"Practice makes for skill in all things." He kissed her once more, but hobbled on his ankle, unsteady and felt a sharp stab. He balanced himself against the mule and Claire slipped her arm under his to lift him, but leaning close.

They resumed their task. Shelley didn't think more about it for a time, more concerned with his health and the accounting of our transportation. Claire, for her part, did not reveal how the event compared to her imagination, though its effect would soon become known to us.

We sold our mule for forty francs and the saddle for sixteen francs, and bought an open *voiture* that went on four wheels, for five napoleons. We hired a man with a mule to draw it for eight more, to take us to Neufchâtel in six days. In all our bargains for ass, saddle, and mule, we lost more than fifteen napoleons; it was money we could but little spare. In the afternoon we visited the cathedral of Troyes, which was impressive and the next morning departed for the route to Switzerland.

A curious instance of French vanity occurred on leaving this town. Our *Voiturier*, a large man of hulking frame who slouched at his reins, pointed to the plain around, and mentioned that it had been the scene of a battle between the Russians and the French.

"In which the Russians gained the victory?" I asked, thinking the obvious, and interpreted in his language, as he had none of ours.

"Ah no, Madame," replied he, "the French are never beaten."

"But how was it then," we asked, "that the Russians had entered Troyes soon after?"

His serious explanation was, "Oh, Madame, after having been defeated, they took a circuitous route in retreat, and so entered the town."

We passengers rode in the *voiture*, for that is how the French call a coach, with the portmanteau and small cases on the rear. Shelley I sat together, facing forward, while Claire took a position in the rear facing seat. As we looked upon the passing scenery of nature and man, jostling with the jolts of the wheels in the track, my step-sister, rather than turning to view what may lay about us, kept her eyes fixed on Shelley. I did not make any mention of this, but he as well, took notice of her gaze. On these occasions, she would suddenly look away and pretend some curious interest in the world about us.

This proceeded for some leagues, until it became too familiar for me to contemplate. I instead began to take notice of the *Voiturier*. Our driver was hunched in his seat, an ungainly giant, of ill-fit proportions as if he had been assembled in haste. He seemed to have no care for the fineness of life, or in dress. And his manner, beyond the tasks and communication of his trade, was sullen and disobliging.

We stopped at Vendeuvre to rest during the hours of noon. It was the custom in France for workmen to cease their labor for nearly two hours in mid-day, so that they might take a meal and in all appearance argue with one another, at which skill our driver seemed proficient. Vendeuvre is a pleasant town situated on the watery stream of the Barse, and we took the occasion of our stop to walk in the grounds of a nobleman's estate, with gardens laid out in the English taste, terminating in a pretty wood. It was a scene that reminded us of our native country. The nobleman was not at home, but provided his garden for public view.

As we left Vandeuvre, the aspect of the country suddenly changed to abrupt hills covered with vineyards, intermixed with trees, and enclosed a narrow valley about a channel of the Aube River. The view was interspersed by green meadows, groves of poplar and white willow, and spires of village churches, which the Russians had spared. Many villages, ruined by the war, occupied the most romantic of spots.

In the evening, as we approached Bar-sur-Aube, the clouds made the darkness almost as deep as midnight, but in the west, a brilliant fiery redness broke through. The town, situated in a dale ahead of us, appeared in the dusky shadows, while overhead, roiling dark storm clouds were split by flares of orange and red. I was trying to note this in my journal, when Shelley intruded to look at what I had written.

"Crimson," he said.

I peered at him a moment, annoyed that not only was he reading my thoughts, but that he might correct me. I did not want to change it. He had been taking some notes of his own, which he did not show to me. I stopped my pen and handed the journal over into his lap, and offered the pen. He took it from me, lined through the word *red* and wrote above it the word *crimson*. He handed the journal back to me. I peered at what he had written there. Such a minor change, I should not care, yet I took my writing instrument and lined through the entire passage. He said nothing more, but we both knew he was right. I had said *red* twice and it was not sufficient.

The *voiture* stopped outside a country inn just at the gate of Bar-sur-Aube. Claire waited with the driver as he unloaded our portmanteau and cases and transferred them to the inn. Red or Crimson, there was still light in the evening sky. Shelley took my hand.

"We'll go for a walk," he told Claire. She knew what we meant.

"Is your foot better?" I asked, worried that she did know. But without further preamble, Shelley pulled me in the direction of a small trail leading up a hillside that bounded the village.

Claire fidgeted, like one left out, as she oversaw the unloading of the *voiture* and unhitching of the mule. She came face to face with the *Voiturier*, a giant standing over her, looking at her with his sallow eyes. She nervously stepped out of his way, then looked to where we had gone, walking on a grassy hill toward the glowing roiling horizon..

I removed my shoes to walk barefoot in the grass, recalling my hillside strolls in Scotland, where my fantasies had taken form, yet this was a moment real, and not of my imagining. I took off my travelling cape and left it on a vine. Shelley unfastened his waistcoat and dropped it on the ground, with no care at all. He pulled at his cravat and his vest and dropped them on the ground as well, yet we continued on, leaving a trail behind us. I removed my chemisette and found a bush to hold it, the layers of our clothes offering no boundary to our intent.

At the crest of the hillock, the Aube River shimmered in snake curves below airy vapours of sky, ripped by beams of fire; the cottage lights were reflected in the tranquil river, and the dark hills behind, dimly seen, resembled vast and frowning mountains. Shelley held me in his hands and his fingers pulled at the string of my corset, releasing it over the buttons, until loose, and falling to the grass. As did I.

~~~

CHAPTER TEN

Besançon

As we quitted Bar-sur-Aube, we at the same time bade a short farewell to hills and dales. Passing through the towns of Chaumont, Langres (which was situated on a rise, and surrounded by ancient wall fortifications, once a Roman capital of Gaul), Champlitte, and Gray, we travelled for nearly three days through plains, where the country gently undulated, and relieved the eye from a perpetual flat, without exciting any peculiar interest. Gentle rivers, their banks ornamented by a few trees, stole through these plains, and a thousand beautiful summer insects skimmed over the streams. The third day was a day of rain, and the first that had taken place during our journey.

We were soon wet through, and were glad to stop at a little inn to dry ourselves. The reception we received there was very unprepossessing; the people still kept their seats round the fire, and seemed very unwilling to make way for the dripping guests. The dining chamber was filled with a smoke from the kitchen, and at least some of the occupants turned toward us, curious a moment, then returned to their conversations. Perhaps it was our foreign manner, or they were much used to visitors on the road. Claire stepped to a table of what appeared to be working men from the wines and inquired if they might make room.

"*Excusez-mois, nous avon voyagez un long chemin. Pourrions nous occuper ces sièges?*"

They merely looked at her, regardless of her attempt at their language, yet went back to their conversation. One of them, however, a rough fellow with one eye slightly damaged, likely from some incident of conflict, or perhaps in the field, turned back to her in the most rude of manner and licked his lips.

Shelley stepped forward, in a flash of temper, with the full intent to engage the man, who by my estimate would have more than three stones on him, even though Shelley was soaking wet. Shelley had faced many a foe in his school days; he was trained to box, and always ready to defend himself, or a friend. The rough fellow with a face reminiscent of the duel of cats in an alley arose to face him, in beefy advantage and clenched callused hands. I feared for Shelley, for he did not shrink, until the most curious of causes intervened; Claire opened her mouth as if to sing, yet let out the most horrific and piercing of screams. It was if a spirit from beyond had entered the room in a wail of torment.

The coming fight was stopped in frozen tableau. The men from the table, including cat scratch of the licking tongue and some others wholly unrelated, scrambled from their seats and fell away from the table, to re-gather in another space across the room. Clare gestured to the now vacant table for us to sit.

"*Mes amis, prenez un asseoir.*"

We sat together as the other visitors of the inn tried to avoid looking at us. Claire grinned with a pure satisfaction. Shelley was astonished. For myself, I had seen my step-sister perform this before, though she had not for several years now. It was a version of her waking terrors and a tantrum of theatrical proportion she had practiced as a child, which had been useful to her on occasion for getting her desires when confronted by indifference from her parents, performing it at least once in a large company of friends at a social occasion.

She shrugged in innocence and victory, "Well, it always worked on mother." And we finished our lunch in solitude, till the rain stopped.

In the afternoon, the weather became fine, and at about six in the evening we neared Besançon. Hills had appeared in the distance during the whole day, and we had advanced gradually towards them, but were unprepared for the scene that broke upon us as we passed the outer gate barrier. On quitting the walls, the road wound underneath a high precipice, while on the other side the hills rose more gradually, and the green valley that intervened between was watered by a pleasant river, so that before us arose an amphitheater of hills covered with vines, irregular and rocky. The road was cut through a precipitous rock that arose on one side. This approach to mountain scenery filled us with delight, but it was otherwise with our *Voiturier*. He was from the plains of Troyes, and these hills so utterly scared him that he lost his reason. He stopped the carriage and threw open the door. He waved for us to get out. Shelley complained that his foot was still not healthy, but the driver would not be put off.

We exited the *voiture* to walk as the obstreperous driver slowly urged his mule over the steep road. We had but taken a few steps when the scene which broke upon us delighted us. This was Burgundy, that land which had produced mighty conflicts between its dukes of great historic families and the kings of France, spoken of in Shakespeare.

"*Peace be with Burgundy!*" Claire gestured dramatically across the scene. She turned back to us, reciting from *King Lear*. She had remembered the play to perform scenes as Cordelia for Mr. Lamb from his work on it, in the children's measure. *"Since respect of fortune are his love, I shall not be his wife."*

I looked at the scenery of the Burgundy hills and recalled the theme of lands taken by a jilted suitor. Claire continued her performance, acting in full throat on the dirt road.

"What shall Cordelia speak? Love, and be silent?"

Shelley knew the play and played along. *"Of all these bounds, even from this line to this, with shadowy forests and plenteous rivers and wide-skirted meads—"* He described the scene before us, as if the player from Avon had been here before us. But how could he have been?

I remembered my part of Regan in Claire's youthful starring parlour turn. *"Sir, I am made of the self-same metal that my sister is. She names my very deed of love, only she comes too short."* My recitation was at best of academic interest, while Claire excelled in dramatic excess.

"Then poor Cordelia! And yet not so! Since, I am sure my love's more richer than my tongue." She turned and clung to Shelley, *"Unhappy that I am, I cannot heave my heart into my mouth. I love your Majesty according to my bond; no more nor less—"*

"*So young, and so untender?*" He responded as she pressed herself against him.

"*So young, my lord, and true.*"

"*Thou hast her, France! Let her be thine!*" He took her hand and spun her away, like a dance; then winced as he stepped badly.

"Did you hurt yourself again?" I inquired with a mix of concern and some slight pleasure of amusement as he sat down on the road.

"Let me help you," Claire fawned, rushing to his aid. She slipped herself under his arm to support him. He didn't really need the assistance in my judgment, but hobbled along with her under his arm.

"Lear rejects Cordelia because she doesn't demonstrate her love as ardently as her sisters. Is that right?" Claire posited as if he were her professor.

"I believe that is the point."

"More that she was unwilling to flatter." I offered.

"Then love must be demonstrated," she concluded. "Writing of love is not as true as the speaking of it, and words not as true as deeds." She finished her argument with self-satisfaction, and smirked at me to complete her point. "See, growing up in a house of authors has not been wasted." And there, she came to the real subject of her interest. "*Free love.* Does that encompass three? —Sultans have multiple wives and concubines."

I knew exactly where her mind had gone, but Shelley was now engaged in his element.

"Free to love, but not free from it," he argued. "The Adamites rejected marriage. Blake compares the sexual oppression of marriage to slavery in his Albion. I had to marry my wife twice, simply to satisfy the approbation of society." His argument now turned closer to home. "Yet my passion for her was even less in the second than the first. How is that virtue? The love we worship is not self-devoted and self-interested, love that seeks not to minister to its pleasures, but because it is worthy, because it is true. That is the love we pursue with ephemeral aspiration in our inquiry. "

I studied my little step-sister, in the bloom of her awakening, trying to assimilate his intellectual response to her more secular interest. This was the Shelley I knew. I wondered if she had gotten a satisfying answer to her probe.

When we had ascended the hills, we found our *Voiturier* at the door of a wretched inn, having unharnessed the mule, determined to remain for the night at this miserable village of Mort, which means "death" in French. We could only procure one room, and our hostess gave us to understand that our driver was to occupy the same apartment. We resolved not to enter the beds, but sleep as we could below in our clothes; planning instead an early departure to reach Switzerland upon the next day.

We found a dirty settee in a common parlour on the ground floor. Shelley and I draped ourselves together on it. Claire curled on a chair opposite to us. Snoring of a most profound intensity came from above. Claire looked at Shelley and I together in dim light, like two sleeping doves, tucked in each other's wings. She roused herself and quietly moved around to the settee in order to ease herself next to Shelley, lifting his arm and sliding underneath as if to recreate our attempted arrangement in Paris. Shelley awoke with a start, sitting up to find Claire, snuggled against him in familiar comfort. Her fingers played, though her eyes were closed, as if in a dream with the strings of his shirt. He sensed my waking movement and jumped from the settee as if bitten by a snake.

"What has happened? What is it?" I asked, regaining a half-consciousness.

"Fleas," he said.

We rearranged ourselves with Claire removed again to the chair and Shelley and I taking more advantage of the room of the settee; Shelley making an excuse that he needed more room for his legs, and fell again to rest.

We drifted again into peace until I arose myself, still in the night, awakened perhaps by some distant noise. Unable to sleep through the hours, with a dry mouth, I stumbled around the dark parlour and pantry, looking for a water pail that had been left for us. Remembering it on a hearth beyond the stairs to the apartment above, I reached with my arms not to injure myself. As I stepped to the stair casing, all seemed to be silent and still; the snoring from above had ceased, when suddenly before me, appearing from a shadow was the *Voiturier*, awakened and aroused on the stair. His sallow, yellow eyes appeared in the half-light set in an uneven twisted horrific visage, while his great hand reached in front of my face as if to grasp my throat, to choke me in a murderous rampage. I wondered if I might be trapped in a dream, that reverie of imagination which captures the mind on the edge of consciousness, yet this seemed all too corporal for phantasm. Then, as I leapt back, prepared to cry out for mercy, he lunged past me, stumbling toward the door to the outside, passing by me as if I were the invisible phantom. My heart clung in my throat for an instant as I realized he had awakened to harness the mule for our journey, and as blind in the night as I was. He had not seen me at all, as he wiped the sleep from his own eyes, and nearly cracked his head on a rafter timber.

I found the water and took several thirsty sips, cupped in my hand as my breathing returned, and never said more about it to my companions, unwilling to expose my near murder to Shelley's certain jest and Claire's whimsy, but the memory of a monstrous spectre would retain a hold in my mind.

It was still dark when the driver harnessed his mule, looking rather sour at his short sleep. The inn mistress brought him a cup of beer. He drained it, wiping the foam from his lip. He handed it back and glowered at us with his sallow eyes. At three in the morning we resumed our journey. We traversed a fine forest, carpeted with moss and in various places overhung by rocks, in whose crevices young pines had taken root, spreading their branches to shade those below. The noon heat was intense. The *voiture* rattled along the road through beautiful forested glens, passing near a fresh stream which formed a pool which undercut a shallow bank, before rushing on. The driver pulled the mule to the side of the stream to allow it to drink.

"If the animal refreshes, shall we?" said Shelley, considering the stream which babbled in sylvan tranquility. He climbed from the carriage and hobbled to the pool, where he pulled off his boots with some pain, and put his feet in the cold water.

"Should we bathe? It is hot," he said, and started to take off his clothes, stripping himself completely naked and flopping in the pool. Our driver appeared shocked and annoyed at the same time. He growled something in thick French and pointed up the road, but seemed more afraid of the loss of time than impropriety.

I was certainly shocked by his sudden antics, but my sister, who had never seen a man not her brother in such regard, except for alabaster statuary of museum Greeks, was I must admit, enchanted. To add to our situation, he stood up in the stream to full height, dripping naked and covered in goose pimples, and beckoned to me.

"Come, Mary. Bathe. We're free. The water is so fresh!"

I looked to the driver, who seemed mostly confused. And to the road which passed so near. I was both embarrassed and amused at Shelley.

"Our driver is impatient. It's not decent to test him." I offered as an excuse.

"Come on, no-one will see you." He waved at the high bank of the stream which blocked much of it from general observation.

"I can't bathe. I have no soap. And my silk would take too long." I thought of the effort it would take to disrobe from all my garments, and to put them back on, for the idea I must admit did appeal to my titillation.

"But mustn't we be true to our philosophy?" he argued, shouting from the water.

I thought about it intently, but then I thought of Claire, who was fascinated. What example would I be?

"I don't have a towel." I said, laughing now.

"I'll gather leaves to dry you!"

But I resisted his arguments. He finally gave up and reached to dig in the pockets of his coat on the stream bank. He found there some paper with writing on it, perhaps a poem or a plot he was devising. He read the writing and apparently decided it was not worth preserving. He tore the paper into squares in his usual manner. Standing naked in the shallow stream, shriveled and prunish in the cold water, he folded the squares to make his paper boats and sent them on the current, watching them float down the stream with not a care for the world about him.

The road led to the summit of the hills that border the environs of Besançon and the Swiss Jura. From the top of one of these we saw the whole expanse of a valley below filled with a white undulating mist, which was pierced like islands by the piney mountains. The sun had just risen, and a ray of ruby light lay upon the waves of this fluctuating vapour. To the west, opposite the sun, it seemed driven by the light against the rocks in immense masses of foaming cloud, until it became lost in the distance, mixing its tints with the fleecy sky. Our *Voiturier* insisted on remaining his usual two hours at the village of Nods, although we were unable to procure any dinner, and wished to go on to the next stage. I have already said that the steep hills frightened his senses, and he had become disobliging, sullen, and stupid.

While he waited, we walked to the neighbouring wood. It was a fine forest, carpeted beautifully with moss, and in various places overhung by rocks, in whose crevices young pines had taken root, and spread their branches for shade to those below. The noon heat was intense, and we were glad to shelter ourselves from it in the shady retreats of this lovely forest. On our return to the village we found, to our extreme surprise, that the *Voiturier* had departed nearly an hour before, leaving word that he expected to meet us on the road. Shelley's sprain rendered him incapable of much exertion, but there was no remedy, and we proceeded on foot to Maison Neuve, an *auberge* four miles and a half distant.

At the Maison Neuve, our transport was not to be found. The man had left word that he would proceed to Pontarlier, the frontier town of France, six leagues distant, and that if we did not arrive that night, he should the next morning leave the *voiture* at an inn and return with his mule to Troyes. We were astonished at the impudence of this message, but the boy of the inn comforted us by saying that by going on a horse by a crossroad, where the *voiture* could not venture, he could easily overtake and intercept him. Accordingly we dispatched him, walking slowly after.

We waited at the next inn for dinner, and in about two hours the boy returned. The man promised to wait for us at an *auberge* two leagues further on. Shelley's ankle had become very painful, but we could procure no conveyance, and as the sun was nearly setting, we were obliged to hasten on. The evening was most beautiful, and the scenery lovely enough to beguile us of our fatigue. The horned moon hung in the light of sunset, which threw a glow of redness over the piney mountains and the dark deep valleys they enclosed. At intervals in the woods were beautiful lawns interspersed with picturesque clumps of trees, and dark pines which overreached our road.

In about two hours we arrived at the promised termination of our journey, but the *Voiturier* was not there; after the boy had left him, he again pursued his journey towards Pontarlier. We were enabled, however, to procure here a rude kind of cart, and in this manner arrived late at Pontarlier, where we found our conductor, who blundered out many falsehoods for excuses. We could not tell whether he was merely keeping to a schedule of his own mind, or had another purpose to his action. In further discordant interrogation, it became apparent that he had taken offense to Shelley's action of freedom. He had assumed a judgment that we were of a libertine character and he was afraid that he might be arrested for transporting us. We did what we could to assure him that no like event would again occur, and he with some reluctance agreed that he would fulfill his contract to conduct us to Neufchâtel; I can only speculate how he might have responded had I succumbed to Shelley's invitation. We could be grateful at least that he had not traded away our carriage or our belongings, and left the matter. Thus ended the adventures of that day, and our time in France.

~~~

CHAPTER ELEVEN

Neufchâtel

Our *voiture* halted at a border station protected by a guard of Swiss in colorful uniform while our documents were examined and returned to us with a mark of our entry. On passing the barrier, a surprising difference could be observed between the opposite nations that inhabit either side. The Swiss cottages are much cleaner and neater, and the inhabitants exhibit the same contrast. The Swiss women wear a great deal of white linen, and their whole dress is always perfectly clean. This superior cleanliness is chiefly produced by the difference of religion. Travellers in Germany remark the same contrast between the Protestant and Catholic towns, although but a few leagues separate.

We continued on our progress towards Neufchâtel. The scenery of this day's journey was divine, exhibiting piney mountains, barren rocks, and spots of verdure surpassing imagination; here first we saw clear mountain streams which tumbled in white cascades among bare protruding exposures of stone.

After descending nearly a league, between lofty rocks covered with pines and interspersed with green glades, where the grass is short and soft and beautifully verdant, we arrived at St. Sulpice.

The mule had become lame and the man so disobliging in his attitude, that we determined to engage a horse for the remainder of the way. Our *Voiturier* had anticipated us; without in the least intimating his intention, he had determined to leave us at this village, and taken measures to that effect. Upon our reaching the town square, he unhitched his mule from the *voiture* while we were still present in it. His agreement of the previous day's negotiation had now it seemed, no value. After demanding and receiving the remainder of his agreed upon amount, he made a rude gesture and hulking like a sad brute, led his lame beast to a tavern in the town. What he might do with his creature I did not know.

Shelley left us in our conveyance while he inquired regarding a new animal for our continued journey. This town, situated on the road between two countries of few passable routes, did a ready business in the commerce of transport and Shelley soon appeared with a man in leather waist-pants of embroidered decoration and a white shirt, also embroidered, with small flower blossoms. He, in turn, led a white horse with summer blossoms in its mane. This aspect seemed entirely too colorful for road navigation, and of complete contrast to our former mode and sullen guide.

The man we now engaged was a Swiss who was proud of his mountains and his country. Just outside the village, we stopped for cows to cross the road, driven by boys, in similar leather waist pants. The cows had large bells of brass about their necks and jangled with a jaunty rhythm as they crowded one another across the track of the road, while our progress was held in patience.

As we continued further, our driver would eagerly point out the glades that were interspersed among the woods where the cows thrived, and consequently produced excellent milk, from which the best cheese and butter in the world were made. He was as loquacious as our former had been garrulous. Shelley had returned to one of his moods, seeming by degrees to an irritation as the Swiss continued his description of the pleasures and joys of his land. After this had developed for a half a league, Shelley departed the carriage, and walked beside us; his ankle was much improved, but he still limped while mumbling to himself in what appeared to me a rant about the mundane chatter of our driver. Gesturing at the cows, with a vexed wave of dismissal, I could hear him pronounce one word with enough force to express his irritation.

"Cheese!"

I urged Shelley to return to our company, and our *voiture* continued onward. The mountains after St. Sulpice became loftier and more beautiful. We passed through a narrow valley between two ranges of mountains, clothed with forests, at the bottom of which flowed a river, from whose narrow bed on either side the boundaries of the vale arose precipitously. The road lay about half-way up the mountain, which formed one of the sides, and we saw the over-hanging rocks above us and below sheltered enormous pines, with the river, not to be perceived but from its reflection of the light of heaven, far beneath. The mountains of this beautiful ravine are so little separated asunder in a narrow passage, that in time of war with France an iron chain is thrown across it to thwart advance.

Two leagues from Neufchâtel we saw the Alps, in range after range of black mountains seen extending one before the other, and far behind all, towering above every feature of the scene, the snowy Alps. They were an hundred miles distant, but reached so high in the heavens, that they looked like those accumulated clouds of dazzling white that arrange themselves on the horizon during summer. Their immensity staggered the imagination, and so far surpassed all conception, that it required an effort of understanding to believe that they indeed formed a part of the earth. From this point we descended to Neufchâtel, which is situated in a narrow plain, between the mountains and its immense lake, a beautiful stretch of blue appearing between the steep crags of a pass.

At Neufchâtel, a Swiss whom Shelley met at the post office, kindly interested himself in our affairs. We had fallen desperately low of funds and there were no letters from England at the Bureau de Poste, as Shelley had anticipated, and could not be for another week. The Swiss, whose name was Travanet, invited to show us his city. We climbed a series of steps from the lakeside where the poste was located, in a district which included the road station, and followed him to an ancient fortress situated on a crown of the hill above the town. The view of the lake from this vantage was charming, with the distant Alps silhouette in a shimmering haze.

We visited the city cathedral, with ceiling vaults painted in a deep cobalt blue between stone ribs and dotted with a heaven of golden stars. Our host was a fellow of pleasant manner, and a handsome appearance, who dressed himself in the French fashion, with a tall hat and a walking cane. I guessed his age to be not more than thirty years, but did not feel obliged to ask. His eyes were of a deep blue and he had a curious style of moustache, neatly trimmed, but which connected, or nearly so, to a thin trail of side whiskers outlining his cheek. Claire made no comment on meeting him, but I could tell she was as impressed as I with his character and his manners. He was a native of this city from a prominent local family and Shelley casually addressed him as Alexandre, having struck up an easy conversation of members of a common class.

"Our little cathedral has been here since eleven-hundred and eighty five," he said, acting as our guide with a friendly demeanor, pointing with his hat, held loosely by the brim in his hand, gesturing with it toward significant features. "The south chapel was added in fourteen-hundred and the pipe organ in seventeen-hundred and fifty years. In our Protestant fervor of Monsieur Calvin (his pronunciation had a distinct and curious emphasis for the last syllable), most of the Catholic religious art was removed or destroyed."

In comparison to the great gothic Catholic cathedrals we had seen in France, this Swiss variety was indeed devoid of the statues and illustrations of passion which were the principal objects of beauty and attraction to pilgrims in the previous country. "We have recovered our ceiling, which I am sure you will agree is quite beautiful. And our counts—" he added with some pride, as we stood before a large tomb in the form of a monument with the carved figures of medieval knights in armor, and ladies, painted in rich and varied colours, piously holding their hands together in prayer.

"The Counts of Neufchâtel, a gift of Louis of Bourgogne, Count of Neufchâtel in thirteen-seventy— something. I think I may have a distant relation in the back. Very distant." He pointed with his hat toward a dark corner of the monument with a self-effaced smile. We owed some great consideration to him, as he had assisted Shelley at the banker's where he was known, and had been told to return in two hours for an answer; the object of our city tour.

"Thank you so much, Monsieur Travanet, for showing us your beautiful city," I said, as I was enjoying his tour, and meant it.

"My pleasure."

"How did you and Mr. Shelley become so quickly acquainted?" I asked, as their meeting had occurred while my sister and I had waited with the *voiture*, having dismissed the Swiss driver.

Shelley and Alexandre exchanged a good-natured mutual laugh and at once said "Rousseau," as if it provided a complete explanation.

Shelley could see our confusion and explained. "I was inquiring at the post of the financier Peyrou, who paid for the publishing of the works of Jean Jacques Rousseau in Geneva. I was told he had a magnificent house here. Alexandre, it turns out, is a relation."

"Another distant relative, on my mother's side," he smiled with a small bow.

"Peyrou died a few years ago now and the house has been purchased by a Prussian Count," Shelley continued with what he had learned from their conversation.

"He's becoming Prussian. A small detail," added Travanet. "He was a friend to Napoléon." Then, he whispered with an amused aside, shaded behind his hat, "the Empress Josephine has slept there."

We laughed with him, and found him quite likable. We exited the church, which was dark, and found ourselves again in the daylight. He turned abruptly as if a thought had suddenly entered his mind.

"I have been invited to a dinner this evening," he said. "Perhaps I may bring guests. Have you the time? It is, I must warn you, a formal occasion and some important people will be there."

We were surprised and delighted at such an invitation, but worried that although Shelley was of a social station which might not draw attention, my sister and I were not.

"Will they accept us?" I asked.

"If I tell them I bring Mr. Percy Shelley, the Oxford poet and author of *St Irvyne*, and the beautiful daughters of celebrated London publishing circles, they will be enchanted, I think. We are not so grand here in Switzerland, and our heritage in culture is a source of pride."

Shelley and Alexandre deposited us at our hotel whilst they returned to their appointment at the banker's. We had a suite with high ceilings and a view of the beautiful lake. Our portmanteau had been delivered and Claire and I busied ourselves with refreshing evolutions. Claire searched the bottom confines of our portmanteau, most all of our clothes having been of previous use. We had each of us packed one gown of social quality and not had occasion to unpack them on our entire journey to this point. I was not feeling my best and very tired. The idea of a social adventure in unfamiliar society was not as attractive as the first clean bed since Paris. My sister was another matter.

"Oh, to go to a ball!" she exclaimed. "I have not come out in society."

Indeed she had not, nor had I in any real sense of the concept; the idea of such custom of the gentile classes being abhorrent to father, and unimaginable for her mother of haphazard pedigree.

"Who will announce us?" she wondered with excitement, imagining herself as a princess in a fairy tale.

"I suspect Monsieur Travanet will introduce us to his friends," I answered.

"He is handsome, isn't he?"

"Claire—" I began, expecting to offer her some cautionary advise, but was interrupted.

"Clara. Call me Clara, now. We have been speaking French for so long. I think a difference would be nice. Though, they are likely to speak French, aren't they," she seemed puzzled a moment, "Except that he's Prussian."

I was impatient, "Jane. I want to speak to you about Shelley."

"What about?"

"I'm worried that you are acting entirely too familiar with him. I know that he enjoys your spirit. You brighten his, but—"

"I know what you're worried about, and I think there is a simple solution. We can share him."

"What do you mean, share him?" her logic struck me.

"Well, if you believe your own philosophy, I don't mind being a third," she argued in absolute sincerity. "I don't mind at all."

"That is ridiculous! What philosophy?!"

"Your mother's writings you go on and on, and on, about! I know Percy loves you and you love him, but when he speaks of love," she waxed rapturous, "it seems to swallow the world. I want to be loved. Why shouldn't I?"

Before I could answer her with the strength of my feeling, the door opened and Shelley entered. To our astonishment and consolation, he returned alone, staggering under the weight of a large canvas bag full of silver. We were delighted, but Shelley looked grave, for he clearly apprehended that *francs* and *écus* and *louis d'or* are like the white flying clouds of noon, that are gone before one can say "Jack Robinson." He dropped the heavy bag on a dressing table.

Claire got up to look at it with excitement, "We have money! What shall we do with it?"

"Thirty-Eight Sterling. All I could obtain. And that was with promises." Shelley seemed distressed.

"Did you get us seats on the diligence for tomorrow?" I asked him of his second goal.

"The Post Coach was sold, every seat. But Travanet was a wonder. He negotiated with the proprietors and we have a private coach for Lucerne at four, for eighteen *Écus*."

"I don't know how much that is," Claire puzzled.

Shelley sighed with weariness, edged by the wit which sustained him. "May you be shielded from such knowledge your life long."

I looked at Claire, holding her gown in front of herself in the mirror, admiring. I calculated the hours until four, with concern for our schedule.

"Will we have time for this dinner?" I asked.

"We must go!" Claire demanded in such a voice that I feared the return of one her horror performances.

Shelley was kind. "If we leave by stroke of midnight, we can rest, then, be upon the road."

As we went about our preparations, I was reminded of one of the tales that Mrs. Clairmont had proposed translating of the Grimms'; about a girl who must leave a prince's ball by the stroke of that hour or she might be exposed as a fraud. The story had stuck in particular in my mind that she was the child of a widower, who lived in the oppressive household of her malicious stepmother, and had been transformed in her nature by wishing at a magical tree planted at her beloved mother's grave. I contemplated the similarity with trepidation as I pushed my bleeding tortured feet into the only pair of shoes I had, hoping that a fresh gown might hide them sufficiently from view.

We arrived at a grand house of ornate style with a fountained formal garden of trimmed shrubs, like a much smaller version of the Tuileries. Among the city's inhabitants, it retained the name of its now deceased owner as the *Palais Peyrou*, in deference to his position of prominence in the growth of the city and his place in its history. M. Pierre Alexandre Peyrou had, among his other business adventures, founded a publishing house in Geneva which had brought to the world the works of Jean Jacques Rousseau, one of the architects of the inspirational spirit of our journey. It had been purchased by its present occupant, M. Frédéric de Pourtalès, soon to be the Count of Neufchâtel. In the shuffles of jurisdiction engendered by the wars of Napoléon, the King of

Prussia had been defeated by the French and had surrendered his far off domain in Switzerland in exchange to retain Hanover. Now that Bonaparte had been returned the favor, Neufchâtel was to be returned to the domain of Frederick William III of Prussia, as the capital of a new canton in a joined federation of Swiss districts under Prussian control, and our host was to be its governor.

We met M. Travanet at the gates of the *manoir*, as it was only a short distance from our hotel, lying in the plain between the lake and the upper town. A stream of well-attired guests from what we presumed where the preeminent society of the city and surrounding communes, arrived in fine carriages and landau for the *fête*. The formal signing of this concordance was to take place in scarce a month from our visit, and I believe this had some connection to it.

Alexandre led us up a stairway of brilliant and ornate design to the ballroom chamber situated on the first floor. Upon meeting us again, he was full of profuse and flattering compliments for how we looked in our gowns. I can say little for myself in modesty, but I will admit that Claire stood out as I had never quite seen her. Yet, as fetching as M. Travanet promised us to be, I fear we must have been pale and plain in comparison to the jewelled adornment and fashion of the other female quests on the arms of wealth, even though provincial. How our invitation had been procured was of some mystery still.

"How can they know me?" Shelley asked in a hushed whisper while we waited in a receiving line which trailed down the stair from an antechamber above. "I have not been published in languages that I'm aware. And my name is associated in England, but not published on the titles."

Alexandre explained in a whisper loud enough for all of us to understand him, "I have told them that you are the *'Gentleman of Oxford'*, the name to which you were credited. Your *St Irvyne* book was quite the sensation, or at least the synopsis of it, for it has not, you are right, been translated. To set your story of horror and murder in the Alps and Geneva, our country, has been spoken of, and as we gain our news of England culture from certain sources, the review your work received in the *Anti-Jacobin Magazine* was very much read here." He recalled a quote he had memorized, "*a writer who can outrage nature and common sense in almost every page.*"

Shelley was impressed, but still wondered, "But why would a Prussian count take such an interest? And that review vilified me!"

Alexandre explained so we might understand, "The Pourtalès family were Huguenots. French Protestants. They made their money selling art and building ships. They have business interests in England and have been curious about your Prince Regent who is to regain Hanover in his possessions, and what England will do with France once again under the Bourbons as a Catholic kingdom. They were persecuted by the Bourbons as you know, and expect protection under the Prussians, who now claim Neufchâtel. The Swiss don't like kings and want to be rid of them, but we like our peace, so a new government is to be made of our cantons. And he is to be made a count. And he is a patron of art."

We arrived at the antechamber with a high ceiling of fine ornamental plaster and doors of a cream colour, with green painted trim of vine florets, surrounding painted images of Pelicans. The line of guests were held outside the doors of a ballroom with the coat-of-arms of a Pelican on a helmet, emblazoned above it, which promised gold gilt walls and gold edge mirrors, while names were called ahead of us. I have to admit I was filled with a dreaded expectation. I was generally not comfortable in rooms of social interaction with unfamiliar people. Casual conversation of nonsense did not flow easily from my lips. And indeed, I feared ridicule for our manners and no family connections to boast of, except for Mrs. Clairmont's claim to be the illegitimate offspring of some Swiss noble, who would surely be recognized as a fraud among this company. In truth, I wanted to run down those stairs and escape into the night, back into my private world and my own fantasies.

Claire, on the other hand, was oblivious to my worries, in full expectation of her ascent into the noble graces. She pressed close to M. Travanet, holding his arm and demonstrating a coquettishness of flirtation I had seen her practice.

"Will you invite me to dance? I won't know anyone."

"If there is dancing. I will." He nodded with a smile. He must have found her attractive, if young, but from his manner I could not tell what he truly thought of us.

I tugged her away from him to whisper, harshly, "Leave Monsieur Travanet alone. When he invites you, he will."

"Percy is your escort. Monsieur Travanet is mine"

"We are all his guests. I promise, Jane, if you will not behave, we will leave."

We approached closer to the ballroom, the rich ceilings, parquet floors, and gold gilt reliefs on the walls in a grand hall aping Versailles were now within our view through the doors. Claire answered me with one of the most sincere plaints I can recall of our youth. It touched me with an acknowledgement of the truth of our lives, how different we were, yet still bound by common experience.

"My world is so small, Mary." she said. "Father's friends are all ink-stained fingers in dark rooms and speak of things I can only half understand. They all huddle and argue of Mr. Godwin's dislike for noble society, when it is so beautiful!"

We finally arrived at the precipice of that beauty, to fall in and be swallowed. The ballroom had been set for a dinner with a long table in the square room, seating about 20 pairs of guests of Neufchâtel society. When we stepped our turn to the ceremony master steward, we could see that he read from a list. Until now, the guests already gathered seemed to show no interest in the arrivals as they were mostly familiar with one another.

"Monsieur Alexandre du Pury-Travanet", he announced, engendering a few glances. M. Travanet was related by the marriage of an aunt to a member of the house's previous occupant.

Shelley was next. "Monsieur Percy Bysshe-Shelley Oxford, Esquire." A few people turned to look, curiously. Shelley's fame had not spread quite as widely as Alexandre had intimated, and in giving Shelley's pseudonymous credit for his book, had confused his title.

Shelley whispered aside to me with an amused wan grin, "I was shunned from Oxford, now it seems it is my birthright."

Claire was next. She stepped forward with excitement to be presented and be "known".

The steward read from his paper, "Mademoiselle Jane Claire Clara Clairmont-Godwin." She tried to maintain her poise, while the interested eyes of the audience turned to see a new face, but her indecision of identity had come to badger her.

I was next, "Mademoiselle Marie Godwin-Wollstonecraft."

He had the order of my family transposed. It was a small error, to me of little matter, and I expected of no interest to anyone else, except that with its reading aloud, suddenly a number of guests, mostly women, turned their heads sharply with curiosity. A hushed whisper seemed to circle the room, gaining force as it passed, and more of the women, in their glittering jewels turned to peer at me. They shifted position for better view of me and those with fans dropped them.

First one, then another, and then a few more stepped toward me, with brightening faces of expectant warmth and interest. Why would they notice me? I had no fame, no wealth, no spectacular beauty or politic. Yet, as they surged toward me, as if I were a magnet, I heard the whispers more clearly. "Marie Wollstonecraft! Marie Wollstonecraft!" was the hushed name under their exited breaths. I took a step back as I realized that had mistaken me.

"It appears your mother *is* published in languages—" Shelley marveled.

Now, my breath was taken away; my throat caught with a swelling of emotion. I held my hand to my chest to keep my heart from bursting out, trying to keep tears at bay. In England, my mother was forgotten and despised. It had seemed that I alone held her memory. My father's biography had brought her ridicule. My step-mother was, for most of my life, so hateful of her reputation and fearful of her own that she refused to allow my father to print her books, or even display her image in our house. Petty social mores had banned her ideas of women's freedom to obscurity. But here, in a foreign place, translated by unknown publishers so inspired by her ideas she had been read by women above her station, so touched by her inspiration they crowded on me, in belief that I was that author.

"*Ma mère. Oui, ma maman*— My mother," was all I could tell them as they asked me a thousand questions in French of which I could distinguish only their fascination, and trying to explain that she was no longer alive, which seemed to cause great pity in them, but more interest in me.

I had left home with Shelley, in part, to discover some of the history of my mother in Paris, and yet I found her here present in Switzerland, and knew from that moment, she would be rediscovered by others of my age and to follow me. This was worth to me entirely all that had come before, and what would follow.

We were seated at the table in arranged places, separated from our escorts and each other, placed it seems to induce conversation with those we did not know. I was seated at one end, which seemed to be of some honor, and I did manage some discussion of my mother's thoughts with those near to me. Claire was sat in the middle of the long table, between an older woman of healthy girth and an older man of the business class with some kind of a medal pinned to his coat.

The house owner and our host, Frederic Louis, was a handsome man about thirty-five years of age I estimated, with a trimmed beard not unlike M. Travanet, wearing a very rich jacket and several medals pinned to himself. He sat at the far end of the table from me, with Shelley seated nearby to him. At my end of the table, seated at the center facing her husband at the distance, was his wife, Louise Elizabeth, whom I guessed was closer to twenty-two or perhaps twenty-four. She was bedecked in jewelry and a most fine gown complimenting her slender figure, and was very pretty, I thought. She spoke only French and said very little. She had no knowledge of, nor interest in, my mother's writing, but was kind to me as a guest nearer her age than those around us. The servants brought several courses of the most deliciously prepared fare, rich in foul and game, *consommé* and *croûte*, sauces and cheeses, and a delightful flavouring called a *truffe*.

Travanet was seated across from Claire. He smiled at her on occasion as she was spoken to by the elder folk. She, for the most part, ignored them, hoping to catch the attention of another youngish man, for the room at least, about Travanet's age, two seats beyond Alexandre.

The Count Frederic looked down the table at me speaking to his wife and turned to Shelley, confiding quietly, "I should be careful, my wife is talking to Mademoiselle Wollstonecraft. She may take ideas. She's Catholic." His English was passing. His manner was relaxed, but studied.

"Miss Godwin's ideas and her mother's," Shelley began to respond, glancing along the length of the table, "which have obviously created an effect in this part of the world, while sympathetic, diverge in a number of aspects. Where Wollstonecraft was most interested—'"

Count Frederic made a gesture with his hand, stopping Shelley. He was apparently not interested himself in those ideas. He had made his joke and was satisfied with it.

"Why do you go to Lucerne?" he asked now.

Shelley was perfectly happy to shift a conversation, "To find the Lake of Uri. More precisely, the inspiration of Schiller, and the land of the beginning of Swiss democracy."

Frederic brightened, pointing generally to his head, "Oh, Guillaume Tell. With the apple. And the arrow. Shooting his boy's head." He corrected himself, "Shooting off his boy's head. Rising up the people against the Habsburgs." His interest in his country's history seemed to favor the aristocratic side, rather than Shelley's more plebian interest. Tell had inspired the Swiss to revolt and push the Austrian emperors from central Switzerland.

Shelley explained the origin of our journey, and the goal of its course which he had told to me when we had yet to form a plan. "Miss Godwin's step-mother has translated some of Friedrich Schiller's other works. We took an interest in our journey from the story of Tell, and the descriptions of the lake and mountains sound quite beautiful. We were looking for a place that might offer inspiration, yet allow us a freedom to live as we choose. We had thought to continue onward over St Gotthard Pass, or settle there."

Count Frederic nodded, though it was not clear whether he was listening. He glanced again down the long table, puzzled now. "A second mother? She writes?"

"Who, sir?" Shelley had to ask.

"Two mothers. They both are writers?"

"Her step-mother publishes. She translates books that others have written. Her first mother is dead. The other young woman, Claire, is the daughter of the second."

Frederic nodded, understanding it all now, or at least as much as he needed.

"Ah."

The servants went about their chores, efficiently serving guests used to similar grand dinners. Claire was not. She had failed to gain the attention of the young man she did not know, nor the one she did. She sat bored, framed by those who might have been her grandparents. There was red wine in a stem glass among the sparkling crystal; she thought they might have given it to her by mistake and drank it quickly. Her plate was removed as she finished a course and another placed in front of her. The empty wine glass was removed by a servant and another placed in the same spot. Another servant in livery came with a bottle and cloth draped on his sleeve and poured more wine into the glass. Again, it must be a mistake, or perhaps she was expected to drink it to an express an opinion with her neighbours. She drank it quickly, trying to think of how to describe the taste. She liked it, but nothing other than "grapy" came to mind.

I was brought from my attention. watching my sister, by the young Madame Countess Pourtalès leaning in close to me. She had perhaps perceived my waning interest in the social atmosphere and endeavoured to engage me in English. It was the first indication that she possessed any of the vocabulary.

"Your *familie. Où se trouve*— They are from?" she struggled with a thick French accent.

"Where is my family from?" I repeated the question helpfully and gave an answer. "London."

The countess looked puzzled, she shook her head and helpfully added gestures to the conversation.

"*Vous patrimonie*? My *familie* is from Haute Provence. *La Maison de Castellane. Descendant de les Comtes des Arles et Le Charles d'Anjou. Et vous—* your ancestry?

I understood, she was asking about my heritage, but I only had geography. "My family? We're from Bristol and Bath."

The countess nodded with the relief of familiarity. It was something she knew. She seemed pleased we were communicating.

"Ah, *oui*! Bath. *Oui.*" She smiled.

I smiled at her as well. She waited for me to return the conversation, about some nonsense, the weather or the beauty of the floral patterns on the china, but I said nothing, for she would not understand what was in my mind.

It was clear that she had grown in privilege; she knew exactly the line of her parentage from which she had evolved, tracing to early kings of great medieval houses, and of her place in her world. She had married well, as was expected, surrounded by comfort, and trapped in it. She was exactly the antithesis of all my mother had argued against and the example of that class and its structures that my father vilified. I thought she was sweet, but I didn't have any faith our friendship would last much farther than its present state.

A guest opposite to the count leaned over toward Shelley. He seemed a man of letters, with an opportunity to question an author.

"Monsieur Oxford, in your book—an outcast from society wanders in the Alps Mountains hoping for death. This is *Wolfstein*," he began, giving the synopsis and the main character's name to the author as if he might have forgotten it. "He encounters an alchemist, the *Rosicrucian*, who promises him the elixir of life if his magic can raise the corpse of his dead lover, *Magalena*, from her tomb. But to do this, he must denounce his faith and deny his creator. They are struck by lightning and they are destroyed."

Shelley waited for the question, "Yes?"

"I have two questions," said the lettered guest.

"Yes?"

"You, yourself, denounce God. Will you be destroyed?"

Shelley gave the profound question due consideration and answered honestly, as an author true to his philosophy and a man expecting his own early death, "Surely."

The guest thought about the weight of that burden, nodding his head in revelation.

Shelley prodded him, "Your second question?"

"Will you visit Geneva?"

"Not this trip."

The guest seemed satisfied.

Claire continued to drink the wine from a glass that the serving attendant was not allowed to remain empty, unless instructed to do so. Another course was served. Claire turned her attention once again to the handsome youngish man she did not know and to Travanet, then back again. When the wine of copious amount began to take effect, she imagined fancies of having gained both their interests, picturing pistol duels on the balcony, or perhaps a sword fight on the *Capulet* square. Finally, she turned to the older companions beside her, now believing them to be her *confidantes.* She included them both in her thoughts, aloud.

"They are flirting with me. You see?" She pointed toward the young men she was thinking of. The old pair had no conception of what she was saying at first, but as her blurry gaze came to fix on the objects of her intent, they understood.

"Him, and certainly him! See how they look at me?" But they were not. The old pair smiled at the privilege of being young.

"Perhaps," she slurred with assurance, "Perhaps, I should have them both! And then see what they think!"

The old man and woman were aghast.

Claire suddenly stood up, napkin and silverware flying. Unsteady on her feet, she held out her arms like a child and announced, "I want to dance!"

She stood at her chair in place, but no-one appeared to want to dance with her. So, she began to sing, in her sweet voice, but with difficulty finding a key, a lilting tune she knew. The guests around the table all stared at once.

I tried to meet Shelley's attention at the far end of the table, but I didn't know what to do, even though I could see disaster. Claire's singing turned to humming; she pushed away from the table and began to dance drunkenly around the ballroom, spinning and catching glimpses of herself in the mirrors. She hummed and danced, spinning herself dizzy, while the transfixed chamber of society observed her in astonishment.

It was at that moment the evening's scheduled festivities had reached the zenith, as the Butler rolled a cart through the door, and toward the table with a large cake for dessert, a *gateau*. The cake was in the shape of a Pelican, the Pourtalès family crest, to be vested in the count's coat-of-arms upon signing of the concord, with cream coloured frosting over a fruit compote center, and swirls of green, to be carved for the guests and served on crystal plates in the shape of a lily leaf.

Claire spun one last whirl, then tripped and fell. Dizzy and losing her conscious grasp on the world, she landed face first in the Pelican cake and crashed in blackness to the floor.

It was the early pre-dawn hour. An enclosed post-coach waited at the stop where the old town met the lake shore. The dawning sky and moonlight reflected in the mirror-still water while our portmanteau was hoisted onto the top, with M. Travanet directing the driver. Shelley and I had changed into our regular travelling clothes again. Claire was also changed, with the assistance of a *femme de chambre* of the hotel, aroused from sleep for the purpose and given the five silver *écus* for it, not by us, but by Alexandre, exacting a promise from the girl that she could not recall anything from that night but a deep sleep.

The coach was arranged for four, but with packing and the difficulties with Claire, who would rouse long enough to expurgate meal courses, and then collapse again for a progressed time before the next awakening, we departed from Neufchâtel at six. Our Swiss friend, in pure kindness, accompanied us a little way out of town.

Claire remained crumpled asleep as the morning rays pierced the closed shade of the coach. I rode next to her, satisfied that she seemed at last comfortable. Shelley and Travanet rode opposite to us. I caught them in their smiles of amusement, and they stopped. Alexandre should have been furious with us for such behavior in his environment where he must continue in commerce with the society in witness, but he was the picture of generosity.

With Claire settled, and my own mind filled with new experience, I reached to find my journal paper and quill, thinking to jot some details before I, too, drifted into delayed sleep.

"What do you write?" It was Alexandre asking.

"Mary has been keeping a journal of our travels," Shelley explained. "I have been taking a few notes as well. She was thinking it might make for a story to publish, if any events were worthy of an interesting feature."

Travanet seemed to turn a shade of pale. "I would be so grateful if you would not write of the Count Pourtalès. We are in a delicate negotiation with the Prussian court and, uh, many other—entities."

I realized. "Of course," and put away my paper again.

He held a finger to his lip as if thinking. He looked to Shelley and then back to me. "I would beg of you—"

"Yes," Shelley said, expecting what he might ask.

"If you would never make reference to this evening, to anyone who may know the count—the English court of your Prince Regent, especially, while the House of Hanover—indeed the Prussian kingdom, survives."

"You mean, forever?" said Shelley, helpfully.

"Well, yes, unless of course we all lose our heads in another revolution," he laughed, a little nervously.

"Yes, of course. You have been so kind to us, Monsieur," I said. "And we have traded you with disservice."

He smiled, looking at my sleeping sister with a surprising warmth. "No. No," he said, "It has been entertaining."

The coach stopped and the driver pounded on the roof.

Travanet opened the door. "This is me. *Merci. Et bon voyage.*" He took my hand and kissed it, then stepped from the coach. He stood outside the door and tipped his hat to Shelley, then signaled to the driver. The coach lurched and he was gone. I have kept this to myself, but if there were a man, not Shelley, who might entice me to exercise that feature of our professed ideology for the right of a woman to freely choose her lovers without restriction, Travanet would have been the model—but the carriage had left the ball.

Shelley raised the curtain opposite to the lake. I looked, too. There on a hillside, just catching the glow of the sunrise against a cobalt sky, still a twinkle with morning stars, was a large house in the trees, with stone steps from the road along the shore line.

"I still owe him money," Shelley said.

"We have his address?" I asked, not remembering if we had.

"The bank has it."

"Then, we can write to him." I said, even as it occurred to me that he had not even demanded repayment, for I am sure that he gave the bank his personal guarantee for the living expense we took with us. I reached to dig out my journal.

"What are you writing?" Shelley asked, worried.

"Of our wonderful stop in Neufchâtel," I said, plainly. I opened my journal to the place where I had stopped. I dipped the quill and wrote in it, "*We arrive at Neufchâtel and sleep.*" I closed it again and shut my eyes so that I might.

~~~

CHAPTER TWELVE

Soleure

The coach rattled and bumped along, while outside a mist seemed to envelope the lake and a fog filled the air, with only grey mists allowing some suggestion of passing scenery. My stomach was greatly unsettled. The seats of the coach were harder than that which had brought us across France. We had we sold it at Neufchâtel in bargain for this portion of our trip costing eighteen *écus* with the exchange. I tried to write, adding some minor detail to Neufchâtel to explain in some acceptable construction Shelley's finance of this part of our journey and the arranging of our conveyance to Lucerne, with the barest of mention of our friend as a helpful Swiss.

"Are you really intent on venturing to the Gotthard Pass?" I asked Shelley. "My stomach is as tormented as if we were a boat at sea." Our plan had been from the outset to find some place of solace in the lands of Uri and its lakes and mountains we had heard as being as far from the world as Milton's Paradise and in which we might recreate our lives as Adam and

Eve. Where we might start the world anew as Prometheus had stolen fire from the Gods to enlightened man, but like that being of myth, we would face the punishment.

"Our finances may not allow us further." he answered, acknowledging the central nature of our situation. The costs of our travel and lodging had been of greater weight than Shelley's calculations of his ability, and the distance from those upon whom he relied had made the procuring of sufficient balance more difficult.

"You might get your wish of a rest and contemplation. If only to keep Jane from wreaking terror upon society," he joked to disguise his worry. Shelley had been teased by the thought of continuing on across the high pass when free from snow in the summer warmth to Italy, but I was so weary of wheeled machines.

"Then let us settle. You could start a romance," I suggested, encouraging him. He had abandoned writing of any serious nature while concerned with the welfare of two waifs he had taken as his responsibility. "You could explore more of desperate monks and unholy dark tombs. Or discover some local legend to inspire you."

Claire awoke, as if having head the siren call of her name. She stretched herself like a cat, the effect of a long sleep seeming to have removed most of the remaining effect of wine. She looked out the window at the foggy mist.

"Are we back to England?" she asked.

"We go to Lucerne and Uri," said Shelley.

Then she remembered, "The ball!" But not with a compete memory, "Did I enjoy myself? I remember dancing. My head swims."

"You danced in the arms of Orpheus—" Shelley waxed lyrical. "You sang in the chords of Calliope and soared on the gossamer wings of—a pelican." He laughed at himself. I was less amused by my sister's behaviour than my companion.

"Shelley—" I scolded him, then her, "You made a performance!"

"Did I make an impression?" she asked in all innocence. This just caused Shelley to laugh harder on his seat.

"Yes. I'm sure it will be long before they forget," I allowed.

Claire now recalled the part of the evening of her consciousness and that emotion which had been in part the cause of her behaviour. "At least I didn't have my mother to brag about. Wollstonecraft! As if it were the only name that mattered in the world. They fawned and bowed and sat you with the duchess. I had no-one to talk to!"

"She was a countess, and the conversation was mostly about—nothing at all. Unless you care about pedigree." I said to calm her.

Shelley laid himself over on his seat to rest his chin on his hand, "My sweet child—" he began, and with the patience of a Job, spent the next few miles talking with Claire concerning her character and the *impression* (for he kept returning to that word with amusement with each repetition), she had made and might wish to make differently in future social environments.

I tried to concentrate on writing in my journal, endeavouring to show no reaction to what was being said, but unable to remove the image of a perfect cameo silhouette of Claire's profile in the frosted breast of a pastry pelican.

The journey to Lucerne occupied rather more than two days. The country was flat and dull, and, excepting that we now and then caught a glimpse of the divine Alps, there was little in it to interest us. We stopped at the town of Soleure (or as we were passing into a district where both the languages of French and

German were spoken, also called Solothun), arriving before seven, which allowed Shelley and I to visit the much-praised cathedral of St Ursus. It was a new construction upon an old foundation and recently completed; and we thought it to be very modern, of that aping of the classical Roman in white stone of coffered domes and regular regimented statuary that had become a fashion. It's openness of space and light we found conducive to a raised spirit, but its sparseness of decoration left us with a detachment from its purpose. We found rooms at an inn of the city and supped simply at the *table d'hôtel*, within sight of a case display of stuffed birds, seeming to mock us.

We left Soleure at half-past five. It was very cold indeed with the mists of the previous day gone, and we now could see the magnificent mountains of Le Valais, that district which spread from our present region to the great lake which formed the southern border of the country. I was not feeling well. I had been unable to keep my supper down when I awoke in the morning. We were far from a churning sea and I accounted it to a remaining sensation from my irritation with the rough road and the hard seats of our coach. Shelley was in horrendously joculous mood, so much that I wished for his darker turn. We heard what I can only describe as every description of fowl foulness and disgusting word association pun imaginable. And Claire's participation and encouragement in this, I condemn.

I was grateful for our arrival at Zofingen, where we would dine, and I could sleep for two hours away from the rattle of the coach. Shelley was concerned of my illness, but I was feeling better as the day advanced. It was his condition which aroused my concern, as I knew that soon he might fall in his mood as if from a precipice and return to his dreadful remedy. I would write in my journal my concern for Shelley's health, but not it's true cause. In our drive after dinner we saw the mountains of St Gotthard rising beyond our intended destination.

Lucerne promised better things and upon arriving, we hired a boat with which we proposed to coast the lake until we should meet with some suitable habitation. The lake of Lucerne is encompassed on all sides by high mountains that rise abruptly from the water; sometimes their bare fronts descend perpendicularly and cast a black shade upon the waves, and sometimes they are covered with thick wood, whose dark foliage is interspersed by the brown bare crags on which the trees have taken root. In every part where a glade shows itself in the forest it appeared cultivated, and cottages peeped from among the woods, with the most luxuriant islands, rocky and covered with moss, and bending trees, sprinkled over the lake. Most of these were decorated by the figure of a saint in wretched waxwork.

The direction of this lake extended at first from east to west, then turning a right angle, it traversed from north to south. This latter part was distinguished in name from the other, and called the lake of Uri. The former part was also nearly divided midway, where the jutting land almost met, and its craggy sides cast a deep shadow on the little strait between. The summits of several of the mountains that enclosed the lake to the south were covered by eternal glaciers. It was of one of these, opposite to Brunnen, from which they tell the story of a priest and his mistress, who, flying from persecution, inhabited a cottage at the foot of the snows. One winter night an avalanche overwhelmed them, but their plaintive voices could still be heard on stormy nights, calling for succour from the peasants.

We watched the scenery pass while dipping our hands in the water surface, casting out intertwining ripples. The surface of the lake was so smooth and calm that my usual seasickness was entirely absent and my troubles of the morning seemed banished away. Shelley read to us from the Abbé Barruel's *Histoire du Jacobinisme*, to pass the time in our gentle progress. As we passed through the narrow chasm which divided the two bodies, the boat turned with a luffing sail against the wind, and we drifted to the dock of Brunnen, a small lake town tucked into the crook of a mountain gorge, situated on the northern side of the angle which the lake makes.

We dismissed our boatmen after the unloading of our portmanteau upon the pier. Nothing could be more magnificent than the view from this spot. The high mountains encompassed us, darkening the waters. At a distance on the shores of Uri, we could perceive the chapel of Tell. This was the village where he of the national legend had matured the conspiracy which was to overthrow the tyrant of his country.

~~~

CHAPTER THIRTEEN

Brunnen

Brunnen was a small provincial town of peace and solace as we had hoped, but finding suitable habitation was difficult. We passed one night in an apartment of such filth, my ill-turned stomach returned again in the morning. We considered for a moment proceeding on to Fluelen, to examine a passage to Italy over the St Gotthard route as was Shelley's impulse, but the wind was against us and we resolved to make Brunnen our oasis, from which to explore our new commune. With some inquiry we procured two unfurnished rooms in an ugly big house, the natives called the Chateau. It may have been the house of a noble resident in the past, but was now a vacant property available for hire and had suffered from its neglect. These apartments we arranged from an agent for the term of six months at the cost one *Louis* a month, intending to make ourselves as comfortable as we could and remain through the winter. We had beds moved into the chambers, and the next day, took possession.

It was a structure of two floors with a small attic space, of plain plaster upon the outside. It rested on a sloping hillside above the lakeshore, on a rise above the roofs of the town. Its condition was in decay and it smelled of wood rot, but one singular advantage lay in the large windows which provided a breeze passing through the rooms and views of the spectacular setting. A small trail led from the entrance door in the rear sloping side, through alleyways between random structures to the village square, passing across a small bridge over the stream from the mountain vale which emptied into the lake, while another path descended from below the front facing the water, with a stone pavement to the pier landing.

It was with difficulty that we could get any food prepared, so would have to procure our own from the town suppliers at an added expense. As it was cold and rainy, we ordered a fire, and they lighted an immense stove which occupied a corner of the room. It took a long time to heat, but the warmth was so unwholesome, that we were obliged to throw open our windows to prevent a kind of suffocation.

The chamber was dark and dim. Moonlight cast through the open windows in a slash of pale light across the parquet floor as if a path from the heavens illuminated the means to our intimate seclusion. Caught in its iridescent beam I could see Claire lying in restless sleep, draped across the cushion of her bed. She was naked save for a sheet by which she was wrapped from her twirling and spinning antics, as if it was there she had collapsed. I had the impression that finely coiffed noble quests were observing from the shadows. There was a rustle at the window and the shadow of a winged creature, flapped though the portal into our chamber, it had scales and claws as was the familiar creature I had been visited before, but had added to it a long pelican beak. I was naked and attempted to run into the cemetery which had replaced the chamber, but the shadow creature ignored me and settled on the sleeping form of Claire. The shadow had the face of Shelley.

I awoke sharply to the sensation of someone screaming. I turned to look behind me to Claire lying in the bed next to me. She was shrieking, roused from her own nightmare. She peered quickly about in the darkness, shaking. I calmed her, and she lay down again. It was raining outside; the windows were shut, but leaking damp with droplets streaked in running trails down the glass as if chasing one another as children in a race to the sill. Shelley appeared at the door. He was half-dressed and held some sheets of paper and a pen in his hand, aroused to see what was the matter.

"Another of her sleeping terrors," I said, not mentioning my own awaking horror.

"I saw him. That beastly giant with the mule," Claire said, her voice quivering. "His eyes. He— He was—after me."

"Did he get you?" asked Shelley, in cruel jest. I damned him with a look to silence him.

"Are you writing your romance," I asked hopefully, glad that he was inspired again.

He coughed and I thought looked pale. I could now see that he was wet; not soaked, but damp from the shoulders and hair.

"I couldn't sleep," he said, "I'm trying some verses."

"You walked again?" I could see that he had been out in the rain, but without dressing; his bare feet were dirty with leaves and bits of wet bark. His habit of perambulating in the night while still asleep was intermittent. It had been a significant issue in his school years, so much that he had been reprimanded. In our time to this point it had occurred only twice: once in Paris, when he had tried to procure a hat from a disrobing rack at a tavern neighboring our hotel, provoking a quite comical confrontation with its owner; and a second at the inn at Pontarlier, where he strolled nearly naked into the town square of the city to relieve himself in the fountain there, matching streams with the cherubim, before inquiring of our hotelier who had followed him where he might dine on snails. (It was this, I believe to have been the incident which had caused such an attitude in our *Voiturier* the day following our promise to be decent.)

It seemed we all had disturbed sleep; perhaps it was the calmness now, respite from the exertion of daily movements.

"How do you feel?" he asked, ignoring my worry.

"I seem to be better at night. It must be the travelling."

"We might see if they have a physician," he suggested, "unless you prefer your meals digested in multiple tastings. It has been three days now."

I agreed to be looked after; we both knew what my recurrent illness portended.

The morning sunlight crept down the mountains behind the Chateau. Shelley and Claire set out together to buy some bread and vegetables from the market, and for Shelley to inquire regarding the local *Médecin*. In full daylight and in my mood, which had turned against it, this village seemed a wretched place, with no comfort or convenience of a larger town. And there was but one person in Brunnen who could speak French, a barbarous kind of German being the language of this part of Switzerland, of which I could discern but a few words, and form no understandable communication in return; it was only with difficulty that we could get our most ordinary wants supplied.

The town market occupied the central square until half noon, amid gingerbread awnings and surrounding the water fountain topped by a bronze star, as cherubim seemed a French attribute. Shelley and Claire asked of the town authority if a doctor might be sent to the big ugly house at their convenience. Shelley did not tell my sister the intent of the doctor, as we believed it was not a suspicion she should be burdened with, only mentioning a general dyspepsia.

Claire was in a jaunty mood, which buoyed Shelley in his as they selected some vitals for our breakfast and sufficient to last the day. On the return walk up the trail from the market, passing between the little houses, Claire stopped, as had become a familiar habit when they were alone on their missions.

"I am not a child, you know," she said. It was in response to his habit of addressing her as *my sweet child* when chiding her. She turned to him, pressing herself close.

"Yes. But I think of you fondly."

"How fondly?" she asked, leading to a plan. "Will you kiss me again?"

"I don't think so," he answered, trying to find a joke. He looked around to the lake and the mountains, then back to the alley trail they were on, amused. "I look for inspiration for romance, but you choose the most mundane of circumstance."

"Then you do love me—" She suddenly grabbed him and pulled herself against him. He allowed himself to be kissed.

I had been lying in bed, not feeling well and awaiting their return. I had a sudden sensation in my stomach and had crawled to clutch a rusted chamber pot to un-digest. Feeling better after the violent relief, I rose to the window to feel some fresh breeze on my face, opening it a crack. When I looked out, I could see Shelley and Claire together on the trail below, between the little houses, kissing. He was holding her in his arms it appeared to me. I was taken by a burning feeling in my face and upper breast, a sudden anger which was new to me filled my mind. He had betrayed me. It was my condition which turned him from me. I was furious and slammed the window shut.

Shelley had heard the crack of the window from the house above, the sound in reverberation among the gingerbread awnings and even, it seemed, across the calm lake surface. He looked to see what it was, but all was quiet. He pushed Claire back a step from him.

"We should see how Mary is feeling."

"She just likes to moan."

Shelley led the way up to the Chateau, still keeping our secret.

It was afternoon when Shelley sat on the edge of the bed next to me as I sulked. He tried to put his arm around me, but I was tender, and still angry.

"Don't!"

He was surprised at my stormy mood. "Should I not touch you?" he asked, caring. "Shall I read to you? Some Shakespeare?"

"No! God, no!" I shouted, despite myself. I could see Claire across the room, sitting quietly in a chair, studying us. I ached for some privacy, soured at having ever proposed to bring her with us.

"Alright. Then, *Tacitus' Roman History*," said Shelley, brightly, as if he had discovered the formula. "I found some very interesting passages on the *Siege of Jerusalem*."

He got up quickly to retrieve the book from the next room. Claire and I remained in our relative positions, watching one another. Shelley returned with a thick volume and sat on the edge of the bed again, opening it to read of the campaigns of *Titis* and *Civilus*.

Claire kept me fixed in her sights and with an expression of victory worthy of that unrevealing grin of the Italian lady of Da Vinci's brush we had admired in the Louvre.

I rose at night and found Shelley lounging across a bench by the window of his room facing the lake. His shirt was open as if he had woken from a troubled sleep. Moonlight reflected on the waters of the lake with shadows shaped by the cloying dark mountains. He took a drink from his laudanum bottle.

I was in my night dress and the floor was cold under my feet. I padded to him, stepping behind him to look out the window, wishing to repair my earlier sharpness, for I did not mean it to distance us.

"Have you been roaming again?" I asked him.

He didn't answer, as if not hearing. I took his face in my hands and pressed him against my stomach. We remained this way looking out the window together, watching as the surface rippled in small currents, and clouds transported themselves across it in reflection. I saw the laudanum bottle held in his hand. I took it from him and held it to the moonlight. I could see that it was under a quarter full. It would not last. I raised the bottle to my lips as if to drink.

"Should I?" I asked, daring more than I had a right to.

He grabbed it from me, whether he believed I was in earnest or not. He looked at the bottle in his fingers. Suddenly hateful of it, he flung it out the window. It fell in an arc and smashed on the stone walk below, leaving only a black stain. He said nothing but turned from the window and buried his face in my night dress, nuzzling against my breasts under the thin cloth. They were tender, but I didn't mind. I could listen to his soft breath in the cloth.

"Is this where you would settle your wife?" I asked him

He looked up to me as one lost and bewildered why I would bring it up.

"You've received no reply to your offer? Or have we missed it?" I continued the subject, mindless of the distress it caused him, or because it did. No response had come to the post in Neufchâtel or in Lucerne as we had directed for our contact. "Do you envision a ménage? All of us together?"

"What has taken hold in your mind?"

I was still in a residual of my earlier mood, unable to shake the image of he and my sister, and shapes from my dreams. "Do you want my sister? She lies there, just steps away. She is beautiful. She wants you. I cannot bind you. You profess we have the freedom to love whoever we might and not be judged. I accept this. It is our philosophy. Take her. I will stand aside," I prodded him. He didn't answer.

"You left your wife in professed passion for me, at the point of self-murder, with a pistol at the ready if I refused you. I did not refuse you. But if your passion has fixed on another, I don't want to cause you agony."

Shelley leaped up from his bench as if he might strike me. Then, he paced, in conflicted anger. He finally stopped, and stared into my face, studying its shape in the moonlight, searching in my eyes. But I would not reveal my intent to him.

He turned and stormed out, throwing the door open and thumping down the stairs. I watched him from the window as he ran down the stone trail toward the lake shore. I could not tell myself why I had uttered those stinging barbs. I meant them, but did not mean to say them. Now, I feared that he might do something; might fling himself into the lake, as he had promised in one of his passionate moods before. But he stopped at the end of the trail and turned to look back toward me. I felt a distance between us. I had put it there, but why had I? Was I was afraid? Afraid once the flame was touched, the breeze might snuff it cold?

The following day was spent in a consideration of our circumstances, and in contemplation of the scene around us. A furious *vent d'Italie*, a notorious wind from the south tore up the lake, making immense waves, and carrying the water in a whirlwind high in the air, whence it fell like heavy rain into the lake. The waves broke with a tremendous noise on the rocky shores. This conflict continued during the whole day, but it became calmer towards the evening when the mists had returned to the gorge, cloaking the mountains in folds of ghostly vapour. Shelley and I sat on a piling of the dock, separated by a few boards and a deeper breadth than we had known since we spied each other across my father's hazy parlour. We cloaked ourselves against the chill and damp, but the end of summer felt like winter's turn.

"I'm sorry this is not the peace and solace we promised ourselves. It's my fault," he said.

I was still in a sour temper, but not at Shelley. "The smell of our lodging is distasteful. It's damp and filthy. We cannot make ourselves understood. We are crowded—" I ranted. "I don't know if I could last a season. And I'm concerned for you."

This led us to a more serious consideration of our situation. The twenty-eight pounds which we possessed, was all the money that we could count upon with any certainty, until the following December. What were we to do? We should soon be reduced to absolute want and Shelley's presence in London was necessary for the procuring any further supply.

"I'm afraid I must present myself in person, for any consideration of confidence."

Shelley confessed that what portion of his income he had, until his inheritance, was flowing to his wife. She was to see to her needs and provide the excess to him, but her requirements seemed to expand with the sums available. This is why he had thought to entice her to come to join us on the continent, to make suitable arrangements for all of us, but now suggested it had been, on reexamination, a fool hardy expectation.

I knew he was right; there was little choice. We would have to go back and would face the storm we had tried to escape. But having formed this resolution, we had not a moment for delay; our little store was sensibly decreasing, and £28 could hardly appear sufficient for so long a journey. It had cost us sixty to cross France from Paris to Neufchâtel. The thought of another coach, however filled me with more dread, but Shelley had resolved on a more economical mode of travelling.

"By boat is the least cost," he said as if he could see into my mind. "It's the land transport which has fouled us—or muled us. But we have some luck that the River Reuss from Lucerne flows to the Rhine. We can travel by water all the way to Holland."

Water conveyances are always the cheapest, and fortunately we were so situated, that by taking advantage of this connection of rivers we could thus return. This was our plan, that we should travel eight hundred miles, yet was this possible for so small a sum? There was no other alternative, and indeed Shelley knew how very little we had to depend upon. I felt defeat, that great hope had been lost.

"Then, we are done?" I asked.

Shelley tried to read my meaning, perhaps misunderstanding, that I included my faith and feelings in him. His shoulders seemed to fall.

"Yes. We're done."

We would have departed at dawn, but our clothes had to be laundered and the house packed and set to order. The *Médecin* at last arrived to examine me and had come with an old *Abbé* of the parish. Shelley was displaced in his treatment of them, proposing that one could have died in the time taken to come in response, though he had relayed to his messenger a visit could be at their convenience, and the doctor had taken him at his word. Shelley's attitude was sharpened by the appearance of the churchman who had accompanied the physician, as if in expectation that last rights might be in requirement should the doctor's visit be too late or without effect, or in the alternative that a solemn ceremony of sanctified union be expected if our suspicion was confirmed. The verdict on my health was that I would not expire in any haste, but was in condition as we now suspected.

Shelley ushered them away and went by himself to engage a boat to take us to Lucerne at six the following morning. Claire and I remained to ourselves to pack. She was determined to be horrid. Shelley had confessed to me his adventure with her at the market and not unlike behavior on other occasions when I was occupied, which he said he took in innocence. I was, I confess with the visit of the practitioner and its import, in no mood for fantasy.

"Jane, I beg you to think what position you put Shelley in. He is compromised enough."

"He can decide for himself," was her challenge. "Who are you to claim him? He pressed himself on me. He has proclaimed his love for me. If I have had him, what concern is that yours."

"You have had him?!" I was no longer distracted with my folding of garments, while she was silent, and just went on with hers as if all was a *fait accompli*.

"I have been with you all this time," I reasoned in my mind, examining the hours. "When could you be alone? How could such an occasion happen?"

"You have not been with us every moment. We have been in markets and meadows and alleyways with private corners. Street maids throw their skirts above their heads, don't they?"

The casualness with which she spoke of such things was a shock, even for her. "I would know!" I insisted.

"Lie to yourself, then. It's true. I have known love—inside—and in my soul."

My reason choked in mind. Could it be so? I could not believe her, yet I could not prove her in a lie, either. "You would so casually betray a sister?"

"You took Percy from Fanny. She loved him first."

The truth was painful and a weapon hard to deflect. I stammered a pained excuse, "His affections fell upon me. I didn't intend to turn him from her. I wouldn't hurt Fanny for the world."

"Then you should feel no guilt." She was flippant and cruel at once. "And his wife? You knew he was married. That is your "philosophy" isn't it? That love should be free to choose. So if he now chooses me, how can you complain?"

"Complain?!" I couldn't respond as argument and emotion collided in me. I might have attacked her if Shelley did not return, bringing with him the little Frenchman from the market with some plums for our journey and some scissors and salt.

~~~

CHAPTER FOURTEEN

Frankenstein

We departed the next morning for the town of Lucerne. It was the 27th of August, 1814. It rained violently during the first part of our voyage, but towards its conclusion the sky became clear, and the sun-beams dried and cheered us. We saw again, and for the last time, the rocky shores of this beautiful lake, its verdant isles, and snow-capt mountains.

We landed at Lucerne and remained in that town the following night. Shelley engaged a boat passage to Basle for the next day, so that we had time to explore the city and stroll upon its ancient bridge, admiring the medieval art of God and Devils among the trusses. Shelley was fascinated by a curious device of wooden slats across the fluence of the Reuss, raised and lowered to control the flow of the lake waters into the river to save the town from flooding. Our supper was taken in the *stube* of our lodging, surrounded by painted scenes of verdant alpine woods and prancing woodland figures. Shelley took notes on his romance he had begun and read to us from Shakespeare. Claire remained determined to be horrid.

The next morning we departed in the *diligence par-l'eau* for Loffenburgh, a town on the Rhine, where the falls of that river prevented the same vessel from proceeding any further, requiring a portage to another to continue to our destination. The laden flatboat floated down the river, through thick wooded hills, with the boatmen guiding it over random portions of fast waters, the new excitement of which caused a fear of capsize, yet we knew this voyage was a route of regular consistency.

Our companions in this voyage were of the meanest class, smoked prodigiously, and were exceedingly disgusting to me. After having landed for refreshment in the middle of the day, we found, on our return to the boat, that our former seats were occupied. We took others, when the original possessors angrily, and almost with violence, insisted upon our leaving them. Their brutal rudeness to us, who did not understand their thick language, provoked Shelley to knock one of the foremost down. If this incident were not so unpleasant it might have been comical; the wiry and slender English poet, in his finery, standing against a rough farmer in his stained leather pants, with powerful arms which had surely wrestled beasts much greater.

The man did not return the blow; I could not tell whether it was from a natural reticence of violence, or a reluctance to damage a foreigner of superior class, but continued his loud vociferations until the boatmen interfered, and provided us with other seats.

By taking the rivers of the Reuss and Rhine, we could reach England without traveling a league on land, but we have never experienced this form of travel in such a wild environment; the canals and rivers of our home were principally flat and sluggish. On this portion of our route, the Reuss was exceedingly rapid, and we descended several falls. There is something very delicious in the sensation, when at one moment you are at the top of a fall of water, and before a second has expired you are at the bottom, still rushing on with the impulse which the descent has given.

Where the waters of the Rhone are blue, those of the Reuss are of a deep green. I should think that there must be something in the beds of these rivers, and that the accidents of the banks and sky cannot alone cause this difference. Sleeping at Dettingen, we arrived the next morning at Loffenburgh, where we engaged a small canoe to convey us to Mumph. I give these boats this Indian appellation, as they were of the rudest construction—long, narrow, and flat-bottomed; they consisted merely of straight pieces of deal board, unpainted, and nailed together with so little care that the water constantly poured in at the crevices, and the boat perpetually required emptying. The river was rapid, and sped swiftly, breaking as it passed on innumerable rocks just covered by the water; it was a sight of some dread to see our frail boat winding among the eddies of the rocks, which it was death to touch, and when the slightest inclination on one side would instantly have overset it.

We could not procure a boat at Mumph, and we thought ourselves lucky in meeting with a return cabriolet to Rheinfelden; but our good fortune was of short duration. About a league from Mumph the cabriolet broke down, and we were obliged to proceed on foot. Fortunately we were over-taken by some Swiss soldiers, who were discharged and returning home, who carried our box for us as far as Rheinfelden, when we were directed to proceed a league farther to a village, where boats were commonly hired. Here, we procured a boat for Basle, and proceeded down the swift river, while evening came on, and the air was bleak and comfortless. Our voyage was, however, short, and we arrived at the place of our destination by six in the evening.

At Basle, or Bale, for this was also in a region where the languages of two societies collided, Shelley had made a bargain for a boat to carry us to Mayence (or *Meinz* as was the local pronunciation) in the Hessen, and the next morning, bidding adieu to Switzerland, we embarked in a boat laden with merchandize, but where we had no fellow passengers to disturb our tranquility with vulgarity. The wind was violently against us, but the stream, aided by a slight exertion from the rowers, carried us onward. The sun shone pleasantly while Shelley read aloud to us Mary Wollstonecraft's *Letters from Norway*. Claire had calmed in our arguments, content to be still in outer composure until she might advance her secret determination, and we passed our time delightfully.

The evening was such as to find few parallels in beauty. As the hour of it approached, the banks which had hitherto been flat and uninteresting became exceedingly exquisite. Suddenly the river grew narrow, and the boat dashed with inconceivable rapidity round the base of a rocky hill covered with pines; a ruined tower, with its desolated windows, stood on the summit of another hill that jutted into the river, while beyond, the sunset was illuminating the distant mountains and clouds, casting the reflection of its rich and purple hues on the agitated river. The brilliance and contrasts of the colours on the circling whirlpools of the stream, was an appearance entirely new and most beautiful; the shades grew darker as the sun descended below the horizon, and after we had landed, as we walked to our inn round a beautiful bay, the full moon arose with divine splendour, casting its silver light on the purpled waves.

The following morning we pursued our journey in a slight flat canoe, in which every motion was accompanied with danger, but the stream had lost much of its rapidity, and was no longer impeded by rocks, the banks low and covered with willows. We arrived at Strasburgh, and the next morning it was proposed to us that we should proceed on the public river diligence, as the navigation would become dangerous for our small boat.

We arrived at the mooring to discover thankfully there were only four passengers besides ourselves, three of these were students of the Strasburgh University: Schwitz, a rather handsome, good tempered young man; Hoff, a kind of shapeless animal, with a heavy, ugly, German sort of face; and Schneider, who was nearly an idiot, and on whom his companions were always playing a thousand tricks.

The only remaining passengers from this triplet were a woman and her infant.

As the boat drifted away from the dock, while the boatmen shouted in voices echoing across the waters, guiding us with poles into the stream, I took a fascination with the woman passenger, holding her infant. I judged her age to be near twice my own. She saw my gaze and smiled at me. Her babe must have been hungry, for it proceeded to cry. Without the slightest shame or hint of discomfort at our presence, the mother pulled aside her chemisette and allowed the baby to suckle. I was contemplating this, recalling my mother's descriptions of her own succor of my sister in her Norway letters, where such customs were more commonplace, and no nurse be afforded, when I was disturbed by Shelley.

"Mary, you know some German," he said with a mysterious excitement, taking no notice apparently of the woman with a child to her exposed bosom.

"Yes, from Clairmont and some reading, but not the Swiss kind, which I could not make the least comprehensible.

"These fellows are from Strasburgh University," he said of the students. "I was asking about castles on the river. They had this most marvelous story, but their English is about as good as their French."

The pleasant one, Schwitz, about nineteen I guessed and well-mannered, likely from a prosperous but middle-class family, removed his cap, which was a sort of soft cone of red with an emblem of his university, and bowed. "Miss, mine pleasure is to meet you," he said, "*Ihr Mann* asked of *die Bürgen.*"

The ruins of ancient fortresses along a portion of the Rhine River where oft spoken of by anyone who had occasion to travel there, of romantic visage, long abandoned by the robber knights who had demanded tolls in small dominions at every turn of the river. Lord Byron would so beautifully describe them in his third canto of his *Childe Harold* that they would become a sensation.

"Castles, yes," I was also interested, "are there many?"

"Many, yes" he agreed, with a nod. But Schwitz had in mind one in particular not in view of the river shore. He began to inform us, in a curious nature of communication in the vocabulary of three languages; where one might fail, the expression of another would take its place, of a professor who had taught at the university in the long past, but whose story was very well known there and spoken of in hushed conspiracy passed from student to student in excitement of a forbidden notoriety.

"His *namen* was Dippel, a graduate of the University at von Giessen in Hess, one hundred years before our present time, who had travelled as a lecturer, but he had a curious hobby. *Interestiert* in turning gold from lead, alchemy, yes?" he said, hoping we were following. Now, I knew at least part of Shelley's fascination.

"*Er machte ein Schnäppchen mit der Landgraf von Hessen,*" he continued, "he made a trade with the—land ruler, the count of Hess, a castle in exchange for the elixir of life—the elixir vitae."

Shelley exclaimed, "My St. Irvyne, come alive!"

He went on to explain the darker titillation of the story. "He made it from dead bodies. The corpses."

Shelley looked at me and Schwitz, then Claire.

"Then, we must go!" he exclaimed with a thrill I had not seen from him for many days.

"Where is it? On the river?" I asked.

The young student waved ahead, "*Neben Darmstadt. Zwei Stunde mit Wagen.*"

It was near the city of Darmstadt, two hours away with a horse cart. It was decided that we would visit this castle. Schwitz was certain we could engage someone to take us there. It was a popular legend in the area and students from the university in Darmstadt would gain some spending capital free from their parents by performing as guides to this gruesome history.

As the scenery passed from Strasburgh, the country was uninteresting, but we enjoyed fine weather, and slept in the boat in the open air without any inconvenience. We saw on the shores few objects that called forth our attention, except the town of Mannheim, which was strikingly neat and clean. It was situated at about a mile from the river, and the road to it was planted on each side with beautiful acacias. We visited there a very fine palace as the diligence waited for us, while the boatmen ate their lunch; it was the two hour rest we had been made accustomed to in France.

The last part of this voyage was performed close under land, as the wind was so violently against us, that even with all the force of a rapid current in our favour, we were hardly permitted to proceed. We were told that we ought to congratulate ourselves on having exchanged our canoe for this boat, as the river was now of considerable width, and tossed by the wind into large waves. The same morning a ferry, containing fifteen persons, in attempting to cross the water, had upset in the middle of the river, and everyone in it perished. This event was ludicrously commented on by the Batalier; almost the whole stock of whose French consisted in the word *settlement*, which we interpreted as useful for *capsize*, or to *sink*, or to *drown*. When we asked him what had happened, he answered, laying particular emphasis on this favourite dissyllable, *"C'esi settlement un bateau, quietoit settlement renversee, et tous les peuples sont settlement noyes."*

As if to demonstrate this lesson, we could look over the side to observe in sadness as a bloated body in black clothes drifted past among some wooden debris, and later the wooden hull, overturned and smashed, held by some rocks and water vines. It was a reminder that death can visit the most tranquil of moments.

We left our boat at Gernsheim, the nearest landing for the important city of Darmstadt, where it was to unload some goods. Schwitz found us a local student from that city's university offering his services as a guide, awaiting at the port for that very purpose as he had supposed. His name was Klemper. He was about Schwitz' age with a stubble of sprouting beard, and his English was quite facile. He was studying law and literature at Darmstadt. He did not know Shelley, but knew of Coleridge, Southey, and Wordsworth, and others of our world.

We crowded all of us into a rough wooden farm wagon drawn by a horse and hired driver, who did not understand us as we talked. The hard wheels rattled upward on a dirt track through a thick forest of pines and beech called the Odenwald, which provided a pleasing aromatic flavour. My earlier illness, portending so much for my future, had eased with the passing of days but the boat and river had caused my usual seasickness, which Shelley mentioned to Klemper, should it be aggravated by the horse cart and we might need to stop. Our student guide smiled in sympathy and reached into his pocket to take out a small dark glass bottle, so similar to that from which Coleridge dosed his laudanum, that I thought it was the same.

"If you do not feel well. You can try some of this," Klemper said kindly as he handed it to me.

As he produced it, Schwitz laughed heartily and was joined by his friends. They didn't seem to have much English, and for the most part, simply mimicked their friend.

"Try very little," said Schwitz, still amused.

"What is it?" I asked, as I examined the bottle filled with a dark liquid, with a stopper and a glass tube.

"The Oil of Dippel," explained Klemper. "It is made from animal bones and some 'secrets'".

Schwitz laughed again, aped by his friends, "*Leichen!* Is the secret ingredient. Dead corpses."

He was joking, I'm sure. I bravely removed the stopper to smell it and I reacted violently. It was foul.

"It smells like a grave," I said in half-jest.

Klemper went on naturally, "It is also good for keeping water from your boots and softening hides. It is made somewhere here. It is a product. You can purchase it in large quantities if you have a manufacture. The recipe was devised by Dippel and brought him some wealth. I very much doubt if there is any dead bodies in it. It does have boiled cow fat, tallow, from the bones, I think. It has been used by local peoples for the muscle pains, to rub and aromatic the nose. I'm not jesting you. I bring a little for people who come, a *souvenir*. You may keep it."

I slipped it into my travelling bag with my journal. I had no thought of attempting it as a remedy, but wondered why it might be so like that container so precious to Mr. Coleridge.

Shelley brightened suddenly, as if hitting on a spark, "I've heard of this Dippel."

"How?" I asked, with my own growing suspicion.

"From Coleridge!" he said, recalling it in parts, "And Murray— In his flailing about to find some context for his translation of Faust, he had heard that an inspiration for the character came from this Johann Dippel, an alchemist. He claimed to have sold his soul to the devil for his secret knowledge for the *Elixir Vitae*. Goethe was a founding member of the Darmstadt Literary Circle and had visited, even after he had settled in the east, and this Dippel was born to the chapel meister at a castle called—um—" He struggled to recall the name.

"Frankenstein," Klemper reminded.

"Yes! I was so struck by the flavour of it, I borrowed it for my Wolfstein in St Irvyne."

"Frankenstein?" I asked. I had never heard the name, but was affected by the sound of it.

Klemper explained as any guide would, "It is common in this area, the tribes of the Franks from the west came this far to the river—and stein is a stone structure, a fortress. Perhaps, first it was an observation tower, or like that. This Dippel, he tried to convince the Count of Hesse-Darmstadt to grant him the castle. At that time it was a prison, already mostly abandoned and destroyed. The region neighbors didn't want this. He was a low-born person, so they told stories this mad alchemy scientist was digging up bodies to make his animal oil, and transferring living souls into the corpse, through a funnel."

He pointed to his ear, with a laugh. The other students laughed as if on cue, pointing at their ears.

"*Seele-Trichter!*" Hoff and Schneider both said at once, laughing. It meant soul horn.

We could see a stone tower rising above us through the trees. It was a ruin, of dark rock and a lighter stone on the wall corners. An arch remained with the tower, which had a steepled roof, and black holes for windows with pointed arches. Fragments of the walls remained with steps to destroyed battlements and a chapel.

Claire had been riding silently though all of this, not caring for these stories, mostly her interest focused on the boys, but their attention had been to me as I was engaging them. She leaned close to me to whisper, and I dreaded that she intended to misbehave in some fashion I was yet to discover.

"They're all staring at you" she said, determined to be horrible. "Even the stupid one. They all think we're going to the castle so they can have a romp. I think you should. Each one!"

"Don't be tiresome," I pleaded, but without expectation of compliance.

The wagon stopped in a small clearing which must have once been a courtyard or outer bailey, with ivy and thicket clinging to the walls, which were jagged and uneven at the top where they had been broken by some powerful force. We exited the wagon, with the students assisting us.

Claire announced in as clear a tone as she could, "My sister, Mary, wants you all. Just walk with her into the bushes. The famous Mary Godwin Wollstonecraft, who everyone oohs and ahhs about! Whose saintly mother, long dead in her grave, was a whore! Just ask anyone in polite English fashion and they will tell you! Who ran away with the great Shelley. For free love! He's married, did you know? It is so scandalous! You know what my mother said, when she came to save me, to take me away?"

Shelley grabbed Claire and pulled her away, quickly ending her pronouncement.

The Germans who didn't comprehend her speech, look bewildered. The ones who did, stayed silent. I had had enough of her, and feeling tender about this demonstration she had clearly practiced in her mind, stormed away in the opposite direction. Schwitz, Klemper, and the other students followed me, not knowing what else to do.

I recovered myself and pretended as best I could to be a tourist, hiding a roiling confusion and anger, and attempted to listen to descriptions of past wars, and details of the fortress's bleak history, as we strolled together among the points of interest, though I cannot recall hearing a particle of what was being explained for my benefit.

Young Klemper must have sensed my distraction, for I recall him asking while the others were at some distance. "Do you wish to go? I am sorry, if we have been too familiar."

I appreciated his kindness. "It's a family matter." He nodded understanding and waited. I didn't know what he was waiting for; did he think he should try to kiss me; or waited for me to run away. Finally, I peered around us at the ruined cracked walls, dark in the shadows where the sun did not reach. I wondered at it.

"This science student, the alchemist —"

"Yes?" he seemed to be relieved to be on familiar ground.

"Did he perform experiments in this place? There is so little here."

He returned to being a guide, "It was destroyed in the war of religion; the French and Spanish Catholics against the Protestant elector princes of Germany. Dippel was born here. He was banished from many places. He wandered alone. He taught and experimented, and he died of poison. He wrote a letter to say he had finally discovered his elixir to live forever—or one-hundred and forty years more, as he said, but maybe it was not so good."

I looked once more around at the shattered walls, cloyed with ivy and was overtaken by the thought of a student of science who believed so intently that he might challenge the termination of life, destroyed by his own hubris—that by the artifice of experiment and his own diabolical invention he could replace the will of his Creator—and be destroyed by his creation.

Shelley dragged a sullen Claire underneath an arch to a more secluded part of the ruin. Though I may say she was dragged, for such was Shelley's mood that he might have harmed her, she went willingly.

"What is this?" he demanded of her, finding a place among the ancient stones where their voices might not be heard.

"I just wanted them to go away," she answered in a demure, nearly childish tone. They were alone in the secluded bowels of the ancient walls. Great portions of fallen stone and stepped terraces were overgrown with grass and vines. A wild stream ran through the confined glade into a pond where the stones were covered in moss. The sun made dappled patterns of the ivy leaves through the stone window arches. It was the idyllic setting for a performance.

She pressed close to him, that he might feel her brush against him. *"What shall Cordelia speak? Love—or be silent?"*

"My sweet child, I am disappointed—" began Shelley, expecting to scold her in his usual way, but she had other plans.

"Why? *To promise love to the same woman forever is absurd."*

He heard his philosophy repeated back to him, when his world had been shifted. "You misquote me. And this is absurd."

"Why?" again like a child in a loop of logic. "We're alone in the glades of the Fairy Queen. *Not a breath be seen to stir around yon grass grown ruins' height. Ianthe arises."* She pressed harder against him. He fought for a solid ground to stand.

"If you mean to impress me with rehearsed homage—I will tell you, now is not the time, nor place!"

But Claire had a design. She began to disrobe, slipping from her items of clothing, layer upon layer, as she performed her own recited version of Shelley's *Queen Mab*.

"Burst the icy chains of custom. Arise Ianthe and bare her soul. Until she stands all beauty in naked purity—" She continued to undress and Shelley could

do nothing but stand, wondering what he should do. "*In perfect semblance of her body's frame. In inexpressible beauty and grace, as each stain of earthliness passes away. Her form assumes its native dignity and stands immortal amid the ruin.*"

She was naked, as nude as alabaster Aphrodite, a fountain nymph in the glade, and stood before him, waiting for him to take her; she was certain he must. In her mind he had been longing for her, but only restrained by a feigned duty to me; had he not stripped himself to bare intimacy for her benefit? It could not have been for me at the Burgundy stream, for she had watched us walk into the fields and the forests to be together, while she waited, alone.

Shelley didn't move, while her mind raced with fantasies and images she had pictured and held in her imagination.

"I'm yours. You need only take me," she said as she began to touch herself. "Touch me," she said. But it was no longer a performance, it was real for her in her hallucination as she felt sensations clouding over her, erotic and unbound images. She laid herself across a moss-covered stone ledge among the grasses, lost in her own sexual awakening fantasy as she felt the wonderful excitement of imagined love.

Finally, Shelley rallied himself to some action. "Please, Jane. Stop! Rise!" He demanded, as he bent over her, trying to get her to abandon her self-stimulation, and reached beyond her for a discarded item of clothing with which to cover her indecency.

Such was the tableau which greeted me as I stepped through the archway, with the German students a footfall behind me. Shelley was bent over the pale flesh of my sister, stretched out over the mossy stone pillow, exposed in natural state, her breast heaving with tortured breath and moans, like the working of some powerful carnal engine, stirring with signs of awakened self-knowledge, under he who had brought it alive.

The students, greeted by such a vision of Shelley leaning over the reclining nude body of my step-sister among the castle ruin stones, the perfect subject of myriad Romantic paintings, when one should expect they might wish to study and contemplate it like a museum, instead stumbled away and ran, as if they had been invited into the abyss, and shirked.

Shelley stepped away from Claire, as she was lost to a state beyond reasoning, and walked to me, like a man whose body did not work. He stood before me, only fixed on my eyes, trying to discover what emotion they held, rage or loss, or disgust. He stepped closer to me, so there was no distance between us, and rested his hand on my stomach, as if he hoped to feel what was there inside. We stood so for what seemed timeless. Then, he took my face in his hands, and kissed me. And again.

Finally he said in a whisper, like the soft wind of a summer glade, "—the only verse I cannot improve."

Claire gathered her clothes and pulled them on again while we waited. She seemed to have no shame, or embarrassment, as I would have been mortified to be so discovered, yet she only seemed to register a sullen pout of defeat. I looked at Shelley while we stood just outside the arch to give her privacy, with our full journey passing through my mind. We had experienced extraordinary sights and scenes and had discovered each other, but all clouded by my step-sister's bald attempt to steal him I loved.

"I don't know why I invited her," I heard myself saying. "I've created a *monster*."

~~~

CHAPTER FIFTEEN

Loreley

Mayence is one of the best fortified towns in Germany. The river, which is broad and rapid, guards it to the east, and the hills for three leagues around exhibit signs of fortifications. We had continued by road from Darmstadt, saying farewell to our friends, and would arrange places on the next scheduled craft, with time to acquire some supplies and visit some of the significant features. The town itself is old, the streets narrow, and the houses high. The cathedral and towers still bear marks of the bombardment which took place in the revolutionary war. We settled for the night, and said nothing to one another of our detour, and the next morning, took our place in the diligence for Cologne. It was September 4th.

The part of the Rhine down which we now glided, so beautifully described by Lord Byron, we saw on either side of us hills covered with vines and trees, craggy cliffs crowned by desolate towers, where picturesque ruins peeped from behind the foliage, and cast shadows on the troubled waters; the sight, so replete with enjoyment as I now fancy it to have been, taking all the darker shades from the picture, presented this part of the Rhine to my remembrance as the loveliest paradise on earth.

We had sufficient leisure for the enjoyment of these scenes, for the boatmen, neither rowing nor steering, suffered us to be carried down by the stream. As our boat floated with the current, turning through a gorge of castle strewn vintages, I sat by the vessel's edge with the water just below. I stared at the page of my journal where I had attempted to write of the stop on our tour to see the ruined fortress of the alchemist with his search for an elixir, thinking how I might navigate a scene composed of principal elements I could not reveal. Filled with a repulsed sensation at its meaning, and with a sudden clarity of relief from my pangs, I grasped the three pages I had begun, and ripped them from the binding.

Shelley had seen my action, and asked with a tenderness I shall not forget, "Not to your satisfaction?"

I looked at the crumbled sheets of paper crabbed in my right hand with no feeling of numbness, and with the ease of dismissing a burdensome weight let them fall to the water surface, where they floated like leaves with the current. I watched the papers drift away from the boat in the current, caught in the eddies and swirls as we passed the Loreley rock of legendary siren call, until they and all they contained had *settlement*.

I looked to Shelley with a warmth of love and a subordinated fury subsumed, as I promised him, and myself aloud, "No‑one will ever hear the name Frankenstein again."

As I looked at the water's smooth surface and thought of that bloated body from the overturned ferry which had drifted past us in horrible payment of an inexorable fate, I recalled a more pleasant memory of three young girls on the grimy dockside of Dundee, impressionable waifs who enjoyed scaring themselves with tales of ghosts and phantasms, listening in rapt attention to a gruff and whiskered old sea captain regaling them in his dense Scots lilt a tale of the desolate and frigid North Sea. Spying though his glass on a distant floating shard of ice, he glimpsed what appeared to be the form of a man in deathly distress, lost and impossibly far from civil human contact. He had maneuvered his ship to rescue, but when hove to, on closer inspection the unfortunate prodigal turned out to be only an unfamiliar creature of the sea he had not before encountered, resentful of being disturbed and resolute in solitude on its frozen raft.

Setting my journal aside I had an idea for a story, and had found some fresh paper at Mayence for the purpose. It might be a novel. It would touch on the themes of man's hubris in the face of a divine fate, on violence and the concepts of good and evil, the creation of a monster, centered on a relationship destroyed by willful folly, and would touch on places we had been and things we had seen. But I would break one of my most cherished tenants and cautions of she who guided me; I would make myself the heroin of my story. I began by writing the title on my fresh paper, *Hate*.

The remainder of our journey was as I have previously reported, without substantial change of incident or feature. On the following day we left the hills of the Rhine, and finding that the river should move so sluggishly through the flats of Holland, and wind so extremely, that, after calculating our resources, we resolved to finish our journey in a land diligence. We proceeded to post the same night to Cologne, where we arrived late; for the rate of travelling in Germany seldom exceeds a mile and a half an hour.

After Cologne, we continued our route by coach to Rotterdam through the flat land of canals and on the evening of the 8th of August we sailed from Rotterdam, but contrary winds obliged us to remain nearly two days at Marsluys. Here our last guinea was expended, and we reflected with wonder that we had travelled eight hundred miles for less than thirty pounds, passing through lovely scenes, and enjoying the beauteous Rhine, and all the brilliant shews of earth and sky, perhaps more, travelling as we did, in an open boat, than if we had been shut up in a carriage, and passed on the road under the hills.

The bar of the Rhine below Marsluys is so dangerous, that without a favourable breeze none of the Dutch vessels dare attempt its passage. It was in truth an enterprise of some peril; a heavy gale had prevailed during the night, and the waves, which broke against the sides of the ship, were quite perpendicular, and even sometimes overhanging in the abrupt smoothness of their sides. We safely passed this danger, and after a navigation unexpectedly short, arrived at Gravesend on the morning of the 13th of September, the third day after our departure from Marsluys.

~~~

AFTERWORD

I never completed the story I had begun on that voyage, with that sharp title more indicative of my state of mind than of its content, inspired while the events were still fresh in my mind and my emotions heightened by my then present condition, but in two years' time on another of our journeys together, while seeking inspiration for a story to compete on a challenge with my companions, the themes of that earlier work would return to me and infuse a new richer and darker vision, though without myself as its protagonist.

My story of *Frankenstein: Or, The Modern Prometheus* is now well-known and well received. These incidents of my fresh and willful youth I have now set down in fuller representation than I have until hitherto allowed are a result of the events of the past year. Revolution has once again swept across Europe and has brought to a close those ruling dynasties which had such an effect on our fascination and precipitate journey. A promise I had made to one so dear and whose kindness I have never forgotten is no longer an obligation.

It has been eighteen years since Victoria ascended to the English throne and the family connection to the

House of Hanover, while one of pedigree, is no longer a principal matter of state. France has formed her Second Republic, and the German Federation after the March uprisings has ended the Prussian Royal Court with the signing of a constitution and convening of a National Assembly in hope of German unity. All the principal characters of these adventures are gone, save my step-sister, who has related her own recollections. My health has been disquieted these past recent years; the numbnesses of my adolescence have returned to plague me.

It is not my intention to publish these remembrances, as I do not know the effect they may have on my dear children, so I will put them into a box in the drawer of my desk, to be opened as they may be discovered when I, too, have gone, and allow them to reveal their contents as they desire. I may, if I have the strength and the inclination to relive those terrible events of loss and struggle which followed our return home, relate further my memories of our escape once again to the mountains and lakes of Switzerland, the beginning of my famous work and its revisions, my lost infants and lost loved ones, and our journey in terminus to Italy with wonderful friends, and its tragic terrible conclusion of that one who so filled me with life and love.

~~~

Editor's Note: With exception of those portions of "A History of a Six Weeks Tour" included, this material has not been previously published. The manuscript for this work was discovered in Switzerland, among the estate effects of a prominent family during a renovation, including letters reputed to be from Mary Shelley to a M. Travanet-du Pury. It was in a poor condition and significant portions needed to be reconstructed with reference to the published writings of Mary Wollstonecraft Shelley, William Godwin Shelley, Percy Bysshe Shelley and Claire Clairmont-Godwin, and correlated with factual historical events and dates. Adjustments in spelling and changes in grammatical style have been made for the modern reader in the novel form. The provenance of the original has not been subjected to scholarly authentication and has been donated to a private collection in Switzerland.

###

Author Biographies

Mary Wollstonecraft Shelley was born on August 30, 1797 and died on February 1, 1851. She was a novelist, essayist and biographer, best known for *Frankenstein: or, The Modern Prometheus.* Her other published works include historical novels: *Valperga, The Fortunes of Perkin Warbeck,* and *Falkner;* and the travel memoir *Rambles in Germany and Italy.* This is her first posthumously published work, though her story and characters of *Frankenstein* have been revised and utilized in countless unauthorized works and adaptations.

Michael January is a screenwriter and travel author. His *Favorite Castles* book series is in its fourth edition with the publication of *Favorite Castles of Germany* and *Favorite Castles of Switzerland. "The Frankenstein Diaries: The Secret Journals of Mary Shelley - The Romantics"* is his first historical collaboration novel.

www.frankensteindiaries.com

Made in the USA
Coppell, TX
01 May 2022

77282577R00134